Trekking the
COTSWOLD
WAY

by
Andrew
McCluggage

KNIFE
EDGE
Outdoor Guidebooks

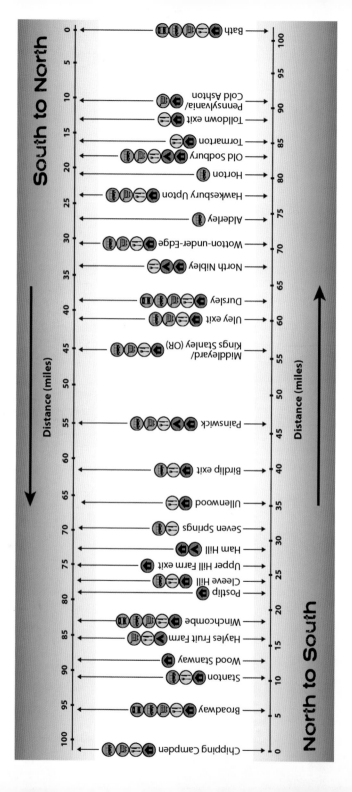

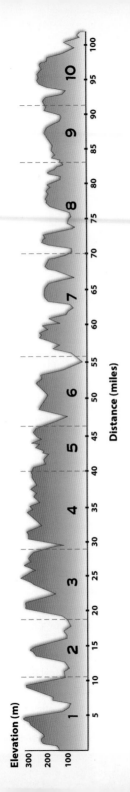

Elevation (m)

Distance (miles)

🏠 **Accommodation: B&B, pub/inn, hotel and/or hostel**

◀ **Campsite**

🍴 **Food: pub, restaurant and/or café serving lunch and/or dinner**

🏪 **Shop or supermarket selling food or groceries**

🚌 **Bus services: may not be daily**

🚉 **Train services**

Note: It is not possible to list all of the locations with facilities in the diagram. Only key locations are shown.

Ask the Author

If you have any questions which are not answered by this book, then you can ask the author on our Facebook group, 'The Cotswold Way'. Join the group by scanning the QR code on the right or use the following URL: **www.facebook.com/groups/CotswoldWay**

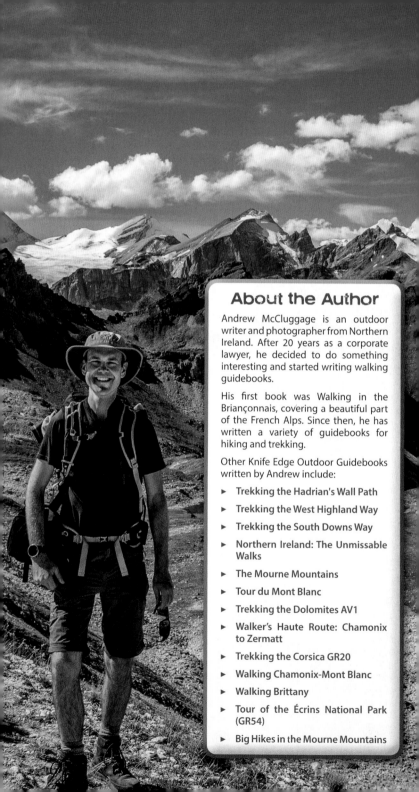

About the Author

Andrew McCluggage is an outdoor writer and photographer from Northern Ireland. After 20 years as a corporate lawyer, he decided to do something interesting and started writing walking guidebooks.

His first book was Walking in the Briançonnais, covering a beautiful part of the French Alps. Since then, he has written a variety of guidebooks for hiking and trekking.

Other Knife Edge Outdoor Guidebooks written by Andrew include:

▶ Trekking the Hadrian's Wall Path

▶ Trekking the West Highland Way

▶ Trekking the South Downs Way

▶ Northern Ireland: The Unmissable Walks

▶ The Mourne Mountains

▶ Tour du Mont Blanc

▶ Trekking the Dolomites AV1

▶ Walker's Haute Route: Chamonix to Zermatt

▶ Trekking the Corsica GR20

▶ Walking Chamonix-Mont Blanc

▶ Walking Brittany

▶ Tour of the Écrins National Park (GR54)

▶ Big Hikes in the Mourne Mountains

The Selsley Variant descending towards Ebley

KNIFE EDGE
Outdoor Guidebooks

Key for Route Maps

S **F** Start/Finish of Stage

1 Waypoint

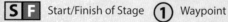 Pub/Restaurant

  Train Station

7 Accommodation

N 0 — 1km

Publisher: Knife Edge Outdoor Limited (NI648568)
12 Torrent Business Centre, Donaghmore, County Tyrone, BT70 3BF, UK
www.knifeedgeoutdoor.com

First edition 2022

A catalogue record for this book is available from the British Library.

Map data

Front cover: One of the Cotswold's magnificent walls (Stage 9b)

Title page: The Tyndale Monument viewed from Stage 7c

This page: Haresfield Beacon (Stage 6)

Back cover: Broadway Tower (Stage 1a)

All routes described in this book have been recently walked by the author and both the author and publisher have made all reasonable efforts to ensure that all information is as accurate as possible. However, while a printed book remains constant for the life of an edition, things in the countryside often change. Trails are subject to forces outside our control. For example, landslides, tree-falls or other matters can result in damage to paths or route changes; waymarks and signposts may fade or be destroyed by wind, snow or the passage of time; or trails may not be maintained by the relevant authorities. If you notice any discrepancies between the contents of this guide and the facts on the ground, then please let us know. Our contact details are listed at the back of this book.

Contents

The stone which marks the start/finish of the CW in Bath (Stage 6a)

Getting Help

Emergency services number: dial 999

Distress signal

The signal that you are in distress is 6 blasts on a whistle spaced over a minute, followed by a minute's silence. Then repeat. The acknowledgment that your signal has been received is 3 blasts of a whistle over a minute followed by a minute's silence. At night, flashes of a torch can also be used in the same sequences. **Always carry a torch and whistle.**

Signalling to a helicopter from the ground

Help Required
Raise both arms in the shape of a 'Y'

Help Not Required
Raise one arm and extend the other arm down and outwards

WARNING
Hills, cliffs and mountains can be dangerous places and walking is a potentially dangerous activity. Some of the routes described in this guide cross potentially hazardous terrain. You walk entirely at your own risk. It is solely your responsibility to ensure that you and all members of your group have adequate experience, fitness and equipment. Neither the author nor the publisher accepts any responsibility or liability whatsoever for death, injury, loss, damage or inconvenience resulting from use of this book, participation in the activity of mountain walking or otherwise.

Some land may be privately owned so we cannot guarantee that there is a legal right of entry to the land. Occasionally, routes change as a result of land disputes.

*Climbing to Broadway Tower
(Stage 1a)*

Introduction

*The path across Selsley Common
(Selsley Variant)*

If a prospective visitor to England was asked to visualise the English countryside, the chances are that he/she would have something like the Cotswolds in mind: wonderful rolling countryside with patchwork fields, divided up by centuries-old dry-stone walls; historic chocolate-box villages, largely unchanged for centuries, with an assortment of cottages and other beautiful buildings built with honey-coloured limestone in varying shades and hues; and green hills and escarpments providing perfectly situated vantage points for gazing down leisurely at the delights on offer. The Cotswolds are the very essence of the traditional England that you see in the movies or read about in classical novels. But unlike fiction, they are real, displayed in perfect order and waiting to be explored. And the Cotswold Way (CW) provides the perfect medium for their exploration.

The CW is one of England's official 'National Trails' and it is utterly unique. It is a 102-mile hiking route which weaves its way through many of the finest parts of the stunning Cotswolds Area of Outstanding Natural Beauty. It follows the western flank of the Cotswold Edge (a high escarpment overlooking the Vale of Evesham and the River Severn) as it travels between Chipping Campden in the north and the City of Bath in the south. On the way, it passes through some of the most beautiful countryside in England and some of its finest villages, including Broadway, Stanton and Painswick. The market town of Chipping Campden (its northern terminus) is possibly the most beautiful town in a region which has no shortage of beautiful towns. And its southern terminus is the historic City of Bath which is one of England's most important attractions, famous for its Roman Baths, the stunning abbey and incredible Georgian architecture.

The CW trekker negotiates the gently undulating terrain on a meticulously waymarked series of paths, largely remaining high above the region's main urban centres. Occasionally, you will cross a road or pass through a small town or village (with little more than a local pub) but otherwise the experience is one of pure tranquillity. The CW is perhaps the most relaxing way to enjoy the Cotswolds. It is a trek to be savoured and it is one that you will never forget.

The CW is 102 miles (163km) long with approximately 12,000ft (3,700m) of ascent and descent. If those statistics sound intimidating then do not worry: with the right preparation, planning and approach, the CW is perfectly manageable for most people of reasonable fitness. Yes, it is a challenge but it is an achievable one. And that is where this book comes in: most of what you need to know to plan, and prepare for, the CW is here within these pages and the entire route is described in detail to guide you on the trek itself. Furthermore, unlike some other books, this one contains real Ordnance Survey maps: for each stage, there are 1:25,000 scale maps to go with the accurate and concise route descriptions. Because all the maps are set out within the guidebook itself, there is no need to fumble about with a guidebook in one hand and a map in the other.

We aim to ensure that you have the best chance possible of completing the trek. We place great importance on the correct preparation and we focus in detail on modern lightweight equipment (see 'Equipment'). We also believe that it is crucial to match your itinerary to your experience, fitness and ability. Accordingly, we have included here an extraordinary level of detail on itinerary planning: our unique itinerary planner has 18 different itineraries to choose from. For each itinerary, we have completed for you all the difficult calculations of time, distance and altitude gain/loss. This makes it easy for you to design a manageable itinerary that suits your specific needs. Once on the trail, you will be able to relax and fully enjoy one of the world's great treks.

The Cotswolds

The Cotswolds is a region of almost 800 square miles in the English counties of Gloucestershire, Oxfordshire, Warwickshire, Wiltshire and Worcestershire. The terrain rises gently from the meadows of the Upper Thames in Oxfordshire (in the E) to the high Cotswold Escarpment in the W. The highest point is Cleeve Hill (330m; Stage 3c). The largest settlements include Oxford, Banbury, Stratford-upon-Avon, Evesham, Cheltenham, Gloucester, Stroud and Cirencester: they are all located on the region's fringes and the land in-between is largely rural, with some smaller market towns and villages. The City of Bath is actually in the county of Somerset on the S edge of the Cotswolds. The region was designated as an Area of Outstanding Natural Beauty (AONB) in 1966 and is the largest AONB in the UK.

The common thread which draws the various parts of the Cotswolds together is a geological one: the surface rock is mainly oolitic limestone, a sedimentary rock formed in the Jurassic Age which is rich in fossils. It is golden in colour and its presence is seemingly everywhere: historically most of the old buildings, bridges and walls in the Cotswolds were built using the stone found locally. These structures tend to vary slightly in shade and hue depending upon the exact geographical location of the relevant quarry. As a rule of thumb, the golden or honey colour is deepest in the N and fades gradually to white in the S. The colour differences are noticeable on the CW: for example, the buildings in Chipping Campden in the N are a deep honey colour and those in Painswick (much further S) are a pale shade of beige. The dry-stone walls, which are a regular companion on many parts of the trail, also vary in colour: it is estimated that there are around 4,000 miles of them in the Cotswolds.

As well as shaping the architecture of the region, geology has left its mark on the local ecosystem too: limestone promotes the formation of rare grasslands that are home to countless wild-flowers, butterflies and birds. On the CW, you will cross many such areas of unimproved limestone grassland.

How hard is the CW?

Notwithstanding the challenges, thousands of hikers walk the full length of the CW each year. It is therefore an achievable endeavour. However, each day you will need to walk a significant distance across undulating terrain so a reasonable level of fitness is required. That said, the CW has much less climbing and descending than many other treks and it is considered to be one of the easiest multi-day hikes in the UK. In fact, there are only about 12,000ft (3,700m) of ascent and descent on the entire trek and these are relatively well spread out across the length of the route.

For the most part, the CW uses clear paths and tracks which are simple to negotiate. There are also some short sections along minor roads. The route is well marked. Most people walk the CW in eight to ten days. However, fit and experienced hikers can finish it in seven days or less and endurance runners often do it even faster. Others prefer to walk more slowly and take 11 or 12 days, soaking up all of the delights on offer, lingering over packed lunches whilst savouring the magnificent views from the Cotswold Escarpment, strolling through the exquisite villages and enjoying the real ale in the country pubs along the way. There is plenty of accommodation on, or near, the trail so it is simple to plan daily distances to suit your requirements.

Direction and start/finish points

The CW runs between Chipping Campden in the N and the City of Bath in the S. As you can hike it in either direction, this book caters for both S-N and N-S trekkers: full route descriptions and nine different itineraries are provided for each approach. The numbered waypoints on the real maps make the route easy to follow in either direction.

The question of direction has no definitive answer. Traditionally, people walk N-S and there are some good reasons for that. Firstly, for those not used to multi-day hiking, it is sensible to start the trek with a few short stages and finish with the longer ones. Sections 1 and 2 at the N end of the trail (between Chipping Campden and Winchcombe) are easy to split because there are plenty of lovely villages with accommodation on this stretch. This means that you can start with shorter days giving your body a more gentle introduction to the trail. On the other hand, Section 10, at the S end of the trail (between Cold Ashton and Bath) is difficult to split because there is no accommodation mid-section and is therefore normally hiked in one day. Accordingly, many prefer to walk Section 10 at the end of the trek when they are 'trail-hardened' rather than at the start of it when their legs have not yet become accustomed to the rigours of daily walking. In short, N-S trekkers will find it easier to plan a balanced route, starting with short slow days and gradually increasing the difficulty. S-N hikers, on the other hand, have no choice but to begin with the long Section 10.

Secondly, finishing a long-distance trek should be euphoric and an arrival into Bath is a suitable climax to an incredible trek. Upon completion of your journey, it is lovely to relax in a comfortable hotel with the option of venturing out to some of the city's famous attractions, such as the Roman Baths. The numerous bars and restaurants in Bath allow for an exuberant victory celebration: the number of pubs and restaurants in Chipping Campden is only a small fraction of the number in Bath. Furthermore, Bath is probably a more convenient place to finish: as there are numerous travel options, it is easier to arrange an exit from there than from Chipping Campden.

Thirdly, Chipping Campden is at a higher altitude than Bath so N-S trekkers have slightly less climbing than those travelling S-N: the difference is only a shade over 100m but at the end of a 102 mile hike you might think that is significant! Finally, as most walkers travel

N-S, that is probably the more sociable approach: you are more likely to bump into the same people each day making it easier to develop trail friendships.

However, there are also some compelling reasons for hiking S-N. Firstly, there is wind direction to consider: the prevailing winds in the UK are from the SW or W. So, if you walk S-N, there is a higher probability that the wind will be on your back: you expend less energy walking away from the wind. That said, there are no guarantees when it comes to the elements. Furthermore, it is fair to say that the CW has more twists and turns than a bowl of spaghetti so you are never going to have the wind on your back at all times anyway.

Secondly, the settlements of Stanton, Broadway and Chipping Campden on Section 1 are highlights of the trek and for S-N hikers are a wonderful climax to an amazing journey. N-S trekkers, on the other hand, will pass these key attractions on the first or second day (before they have found rhythm and fitness) and will be less able to relax and enjoy them. Although it is much smaller than Bath, and has fewer facilities, Chipping Campden is a great place to finish. It is lovely to be able to relax and soak in the atmosphere of the town: N-S trekkers tend to rush away from it on their first day.

Hiking shorter sections of the CW

Walking the CW in one go is a wonderful experience but there are other ways to enjoy this incredible trail. If you do not wish to walk the entire route, it is possible to walk shorter sections of it. There are numerous escape/access points along the route where you could leave or join the trek using public transport or taxis: see 'Secondary trail-heads'. You could start at any of these places and walk a few sections. Or you could skip sections by leaving the route at one of these points.

Furthermore, a great many people prefer to hike the CW in day-long sections using public transport to travel to/from the start and finish points: see 'Public transport along the CW'. Over the course of months or years, they will eventually complete the entire trek. Many others have no desire to walk the CW in its entirety and simply want to experience a few of its highlights. The Itinerary Planner should help you to plan day-walks along the CW. Often day-walkers hike in groups, leaving a car at each end of their route.

Guided tours, self-guided tours or independent walking?

A frequently asked question is whether to walk independently or with an organised group. The answer is a personal one, depending upon your own particular circumstances and requirements. For many, the decision to organise the trek themselves, and to walk independently, can be almost life-changing, opening the door for other challenges in the future. There is much satisfaction to be gained from planning and navigating a trek yourself and the sense of achievement on completion is to be savoured.

However, the independent trekker usually carries a full pack and is responsible for all daily decisions such as pacing, which way to go at junctions, when to stock up with food and water, and choice of route in bad weather. For some, this will be too great a burden on top of the physical effort required simply to walk the route. For those walkers, a guided group is a great solution: the tour company typically organises food, accommodation and (if possible) transfer of luggage each night. And the guide makes all the decisions, enabling the walker to concentrate on the walking. There are a few tour companies operating guided trips on the CW but you should check whether they cover the full official route or just some of the highlights.

Self-guided tours are much more popular and are a sensible middle-ground. The tour company books all the accommodation and provides all the advice and information required to complete the trek. However, you will walk the trail without a guide. Normally, your breakfast will be provided and you can request packed lunches. For evening meals, they will usually provide details of pubs and restaurants which are walking distance from your accommodation. Often, they can transfer your baggage to your accommodation each night so you only need to carry a small day-pack on the trail.

There are also some businesses offering accommodation booking services only: they do not offer advice on the trek itself. In fact, these days there are so many self-guided tour companies and accommodation booking services that some of the accommodation along the CW is block-booked months in advance. At peak times, this makes it harder for the independent trekker to secure first choice accommodation unless booked well in advance. As a result, many confident trekkers (who would be perfectly capable of walking independently) book a self-guided trip simply to avail of the accommodation booking service. By booking a self-guided tour or using an accommodation booking service, much of the hassle of planning the trek is alleviated, albeit at a price.

When to go

The main trekking season runs from Easter to October: before Easter, and after October, some accommodation will be closed. However, in theory, you could tackle the CW at almost any time of year (weather permitting). Even in winter, there is rarely snow in sufficient quantities to prevent normal hiking. The relative merits of each season are discussed in detail below but, taking all the factors into consideration, the optimal months for walking the CW are probably May, June and September.

Spring (March to May): this can be the most beautiful time of year for walking. Many wild-flowers are on show and the gorse will also be in full bloom with its vivid yellow flowers and coconut aroma. By May, new growth will be upon the deciduous plants and grass is at its greenest. Of course, rain is a possibility in spring but it usually becomes drier as the season progresses. Indeed, the weather is often sunny and warm and May can be the finest month in England: in recent years, the weather in May has tended to be more favourable than in July and August. Visibility in spring is generally excellent so views are wide-ranging. Early in spring, the number of walkers is lower (except at Easter), gradually increasing throughout the season.

Summer (June to August): this is the peak walking season and visitor numbers are at their greatest. The trails are busy and accommodation is harder to find. The days are long and statistically, your chances of good weather are highest in this period: often June is the best month and August is sometimes more unsettled. Temperatures are at their peak and there is sometimes haze. There are still plenty of flowers on show throughout the summer.

Autumn (September to November): although visitor numbers reduce, September is still a busy month on the CW. As soon as the children return to school, retired folk and those without kids come out to play. Autumn often provides excellent walking conditions: the weather in September and October can be more settled, with less rain, than in summer. Temperatures are lower but still comfortable. Skies can be very clear giving excellent visibility and the quality of the low light is magnificent. The wide variety of deciduous plants in the UK means that the autumn colours are stunning. However, as the days get shorter, it is wise to start walking early: if something were to go wrong, you would have less daylight in which to seek help than in summer.

Winter (December to February): these are the coldest months and although it snows occasionally, heavy falls are not that common these days. A light sprinkling of snow can be a delight for a suitably-equipped walker although care should be taken. However, walking in deep snow is best left to those with the appropriate winter experience and the correct equipment. Even if there is no snow, watch out for ice which forms in places where water collects. Cold months often bring crisp, clear weather and the low sun makes the light very beautiful. A sunny day in winter can be one of the best of the year. Days are short so start early. Much accommodation will be closed.

Season	Pros	Cons
Spring	Pleasant temperatures Frequent sunny skies Good visibility Gorse and wild-flowers Fewer visitors	Rainy spells are common in March and April Ground can be wet
Summer	Best chance of fine weather Ground is often dry	Sometimes hazy August sometimes wet Visitor numbers highest
Autumn	Pleasant temperatures Frequent sunny skies Excellent visibility Fewer visitors Autumn colours	Shorter days Cooler evenings Rainy spells
Winter	Sometimes crisp clear skies Excellent visibility Fewer visitors	Shortest days Can be cold and icy Occasionally, there is snow

Using this book

This book is designed to be used by walkers of differing abilities. Many guidebooks for long-distance treks rigidly divide the route into a fixed number of long day stages, leaving it up to the walker to break down those stages to design daily routes which suit his/her abilities. This book, however, has been laid out differently to give the trekker flexibility: it divides the route into 24 shorter stages which you can combine to design daily routes that meet your own specific needs.

Each of the 24 stages covers the distance between one accommodation option and the subsequent one. Most accommodation options on the route are the start/finish point of a stage. You can choose how many of these stages you wish to walk each day. Each stage has its own walk description, route map and elevation profile.

The labelling of the stages uses a combination of numbers and letters. It is a simple system but requires a little bit of explanation. Firstly, we have divided the route into ten 'Sections' (numbered from 1 to 10 from N-S): each Section represents one day of our standard 10-day schedule. Within each Section, the route is broken down into stages: every stage is labelled with a number between 1 and 10, representing the relevant Section that the stage is part of. Every stage is also labelled with a letter. So, for example, the first stage in Section 3 is 'Stage 3a', the next stage is 'Stage 3b' and so on. Take a look at the detailed Itinerary Planner below and all should become clear.

The Itinerary Planner includes a range of tables outlining 18 suggested itineraries of 4, 5, 6, 7, 8, 9, 10, 11 and 12 days. We include itineraries for both S-N and N-S walkers. In each table, the maths have been done for you so there is no need for you to waste time (and mental strength) working out daily distances, timings and height gain.

Of course, the suggested itineraries are only suggestions. You can shorten or lengthen your day in any number of ways to suit yourself: just decide how many stages you want to walk that day. It is up to you. As there is accommodation at the end of each stage, it is easy to design your own bespoke itinerary and adjust it on the ground as you go along.

For example, day 2 of the standard 10-day route involves walking Stages 2a, 2b and 2c. However, you could decide to extend your day 2 by walking Stages 2a, 2b, 2c and 3a, all on the same day. Or you might be tired and decide to shorten your day by walking only Stages 2a and 2b. With some other guidebooks, you would have to work out how to split stages yourself, involving some complicated maths to plan distances and times going forward. This guide, however, does all the hard mental work for you.

In this book:

Timings indicate the approximate time required by a reasonably fit walker to complete a stage. They do not include stoppage time. Do not get frustrated if your own times do not match ours: everyone walks at different speeds. As you progress through the trek, you will soon learn how your own times compare with those given here and you will adjust your plans accordingly.

Walking distances are given in both miles and kilometres (km). One mile equates to approximately 1.6km.

Place names in brackets in the route descriptions indicate the direction to be followed on signposts. For example, "('Stanton')" would mean that you follow a sign for Stanton.

Ascent/descent numbers are the aggregate of all the altitude gain or loss (measured in feet and metres) on the uphill or downhill sections of a stage. As a rule of thumb, a fit walker climbs 1000 to 1300 feet (300 to 400m) in an hour. The statistics tables in the route descriptions are based on N-S itineraries: S-N walkers should simply swap the ascent and descent figures.

Elevation profiles are provided for each Section, indicating where the climbs and descents fall on the route. The profiles are based on N-S itineraries: S-N walkers should simply read them in reverse.

Spellings of place names are normally derived from the OS maps. However, there is sometimes disagreement over how places are spelt. Accordingly, you may notice different spellings elsewhere.

Real maps are provided. These are extracts from 1:25,000 scale Explorer maps produced by Ordnance Survey, the mapping agency for GB. The maps are divided into 4cm grid squares: each square represents 1km x 1km. On the maps, we have marked the route of the trek, the start/finish points of stages, significant waypoints and the accommodation on the CW. On each map, N is at the top of the page.

The following abbreviations are used:

BCE	Before the Common Era (a secular alternative to 'BC')
CE	The Common Era (a secular alternative to 'AD')
CW	The Cotswold Way
GB	Great Britain
OR	Off-route
OS	Ordnance Survey
WW2	World War 2
TL	Turn left
TR	Turn right
SH	Straight ahead
N, S, E and W, etc.	North, South, East and West, etc.
N-S	North to South
S-N	South to North

One of the many paths along the crest of the escarpment (Stage 4b)

Itinerary Planner

The approach to North
Nibley (Stage 7c)

North to South

Stage	Start	Time (hr)	Distance		Ascent		Descent	
			miles	km	ft	m	ft	m
1a	Chipping Campden	2:45	6.0	9.6	538	164	702	214
1b	Broadway	2:00	4.5	7.3	692	211	627	191
2a	Stanton	0:45	2.0	3.2	69	21	66	20
2b	Wood Stanway	1:45	3.3	5.3	515	157	505	154
2c	Hayles Fruit Farm	1:00	2.2	3.6	105	32	184	56
3a	Winchcombe	2:30	4.7	7.6	751	229	466	142
3b	Postlip	0:45	1.2	2.0	302	92	26	8
3c	Cleeve Hill	1:00	2.0	3.2	302	92	289	88
3d	Upper Hill Farm exit	1:15	2.5	4.1	197	60	325	99
4a	Ham Hill	3:45	6.9	11.1	1034	315	1050	320
4b	Ullenwood	2:15	4.4	7.1	410	125	325	99
5	Birdlip exit	3:30	6.8	10.9	925	282	1240	378
6	Painswick	5:15	9.4	15.2	1125	343	1352	412
7a	Middleyard	2:00	4.0	6.4	787	240	312	95
7b	Uley exit	1:15	2.7	4.3	295	90	797	243
7c	Dursley	2:30	5.0	8.1	732	223	587	179
7d	North Nibley	1:15	2.5	4.0	282	86	394	120
8a	Wotton-under-Edge	4:00	7.5	12.0	925	282	584	178
8b	Hawkesbury Upton	2:30	5.3	8.5	367	112	591	180
9a	Old Sodbury	1:00	2.1	3.4	236	72	92	28
9b	Tormarton	1:30	3.0	4.8	131	40	39	12
9c	Tolldown exit	1:30	3.0	4.8	262	80	266	81
9d	Pennsylvania	0:15	0.4	0.7	115	35	66	20
10	Cold Ashton	5:00	10.1	16.2	787	240	1398	426
Finish	Bath							

The view from Cam Long Down (Stage 7b)

South to North

Stage	Start	Time (hr)	Distance		Ascent		Descent	
			miles	km	ft	m	ft	m
10	Bath	5:30	10.1	16.2	1398	426	787	240
9d	Cold Ashton	0:15	0.4	0.7	66	20	115	35
9c	Pennsylvania	1:30	3.0	4.8	266	81	262	80
9b	Tolldown exit	1:30	3.0	4.8	39	12	131	40
9a	Tormarton	0:45	2.1	3.4	92	28	236	72
8b	Old Sodbury	2:45	5.3	8.5	591	180	367	112
8a	Hawkesbury Upton	3:45	7.5	12.0	584	178	925	282
7d	Wotton-under-Edge	1:15	2.5	4.0	394	120	282	86
7c	North Nibley	2:30	5.0	8.1	587	179	732	223
7b	Dursley	1:45	2.7	4.3	797	243	295	90
7a	Uley exit	1:45	4.0	6.4	312	95	787	240
6	Middleyard	5:30	9.4	15.2	1352	412	1125	343
5	Painswick	3:45	6.8	10.9	1240	378	925	282
4b	Birdlip exit	2:15	4.4	7.1	325	99	410	125
4a	Ullenwood	3:45	6.9	11.1	1050	320	1034	315
3d	Ham Hill	1:15	2.5	4.1	325	99	197	60
3c	Upper Hill Farm exit	1:00	2.0	3.2	289	88	302	92
3b	Cleeve Hill	0:30	1.2	2.0	26	8	302	92
3a	Postlip	2:15	4.7	7.6	466	142	751	229
2c	Winchcombe	1:00	2.2	3.6	184	56	105	32
2b	Hayles Fruit Farm	1:45	3.3	5.3	505	154	515	157
2a	Wood Stanway	0:45	2.0	3.2	66	20	69	21
1b	Stanton	2:00	4.5	7.3	627	191	692	211
1a	Broadway	2:45	6.0	9.6	702	214	538	164
Finish	Chipping Campden							

Suggested Itineraries: North to South

12 Days (N-S)

Our most leisurely itinerary is perfect for those who want to relax and take their time. Days 1 and 7 of the standard 10-day itinerary are each split into two days. Days 1, 2 and 3 are short giving your body time to warm-up slowly before the more difficult stages ahead.

Day	Stages	Time (hr)	Distance		Ascent		Descent	
			miles	km	ft	m	ft	m
1	1a	2:45	6.0	9.6	538	164	702	214
2	1b	2:00	4.5	7.3	692	211	627	191
3	2a, 2b, 2c	3:30	7.5	12.1	689	210	755	230
4	3a, 3b, 3c, 3d	5:30	10.5	16.9	1552	473	1106	337
5	4a, 4b	6:00	11.3	18.2	1444	440	1375	419
6	5	3:30	6.8	10.9	925	282	1240	378
7	6	5:15	9.4	15.2	1125	343	1352	412
8	7a, 7b	3:15	6.7	10.7	1083	330	1109	338
9	7c, 7d	3:45	7.5	12.1	1014	309	981	299
10	8a, 8b	6:30	12.7	20.5	1293	394	1175	358
11	9a, 9b, 9c, 9d	4:15	8.5	13.7	745	227	463	141
12	10	5:00	10.1	16.2	787	240	1398	426

11 Days (N-S)

Day 1 of the standard 10-day itinerary is split into two days allowing overnight stays at both Broadway and Stanton (two of the loveliest villages on the trek). The first two days are therefore very short giving your body time to warm-up slowly before the more difficult stages ahead. For an alternative 11-day itinerary, you could split day 7 of the standard 10-day itinerary (instead of day 1) and stop overnight in Dursley.

Day	Stages	Time (hr)	Distance		Ascent		Descent	
			miles	km	ft	m	ft	m
1	1a	2:45	6.0	9.6	538	164	702	214
2	1b	2:00	4.5	7.3	692	211	627	191
3	2a, 2b, 2c	3:30	7.5	12.1	689	210	755	230
4	3a, 3b, 3c, 3d	5:30	10.5	16.9	1552	473	1106	337
5	4a, 4b	6:00	11.3	18.2	1444	440	1375	419
6	5	3:30	6.8	10.9	925	282	1240	378
7	6	5:15	9.4	15.2	1125	343	1352	412
8	7a, 7b, 7c, 7d	7:00	14.2	22.8	2097	639	2090	637
9	8a, 8b	6:30	12.7	20.5	1293	394	1175	358
10	9a, 9b, 9c, 9d	4:15	8.5	13.7	745	227	463	141
11	10	5:00	10.1	16.2	787	240	1398	426

10 Days (N-S)

Our standard schedule which is popular with many walkers because the nightly stops are at some of the loveliest places on the CW (usually with a pub or two and a variety of places to stay). Some may prefer to take two days over the first stage as there is so much to take in (see our 11-day itinerary). Day 5 is relatively short for a mid-trek stage but the spacing of the accommodation means that there is no practical alternative.

Day	Stages	Time (hr)	Distance		Ascent		Descent	
			miles	km	ft	m	ft	m
1	1a, 1b	4:45	10.5	16.9	1230	375	1329	405
2	2a, 2b, 2c	3:30	7.5	12.1	689	210	755	230
3	3a, 3b, 3c, 3d	5:30	10.5	16.9	1552	473	1106	337
4	4a, 4b	6:00	11.3	18.2	1444	440	1375	419
5	5	3:30	6.8	10.9	925	282	1240	378
6	6	5:15	9.4	15.2	1125	343	1352	412
7	7a, 7b, 7c, 7d	7:00	14.2	22.8	2097	639	2090	637
8	8a, 8b	6:30	12.7	20.5	1293	394	1175	358
9	9a, 9b, 9c, 9d	4:15	8.5	13.7	745	227	463	141
10	10	5:00	10.1	16.2	787	240	1398	426

9 Days (N-S)

Days 2 to 5 of the standard 10-day itinerary are squeezed into three days. It is a well-balanced itinerary.

Day	Stages	Time (hr)	Distance		Ascent		Descent	
			miles	km	ft	m	ft	m
1	1a, 1b	4:45	10.5	16.9	1230	375	1329	405
2	2a, 2b, 2c, 3a	6:00	12.2	19.7	1440	439	1221	372
3	3b, 3c, 3d, 4a	6:45	12.7	20.4	1834	559	1690	515
4	4b, 5	5:45	11.2	18.0	1335	407	1565	477
5	6	5:15	9.4	15.2	1125	343	1352	412
6	7a, 7b, 7c, 7d	7:00	14.2	22.8	2097	639	2090	637
7	8a, 8b	6:30	12.7	20.5	1293	394	1175	358
8	9a, 9b, 9c, 9d	4:15	8.5	13.7	745	227	463	141
9	10	5:00	10.1	16.2	787	240	1398	426

8 Days (N-S)

Days 7 to 9 of the 9-day itinerary are squeezed into two longer days.

Day	Stages	Time (hr)	Distance		Ascent		Descent	
			miles	km	ft	m	ft	m
1	1a, 1b, 2a	5:30	12.5	20.1	1299	396	1394	425
2	2b, 2c, 3a, 3b	6:00	11.5	18.5	1673	510	1181	360
3	3c, 3d, 4a	6:00	11.4	18.4	1532	467	1663	507
4	4b, 5	5:45	11.2	18.0	1335	407	1565	477
5	6	5:15	9.4	15.2	1125	343	1352	412
6	7a, 7b, 7c, 7d	7:00	14.2	22.8	2097	639	2090	637
7	8a, 8b, 9a	7:30	14.9	23.9	1529	466	1266	386
8	9b, 9c, 9d, 10	8:15	16.5	26.5	1296	395	1768	539

7 Days (N-S)

For fit hikers. A tough but well-balanced itinerary. The first two days are comparatively easier giving your body time to warm up. The remaining five days are long.

Day	Stages	Time (hr)	Distance		Ascent		Descent	
			miles	km	ft	m	ft	m
1	1a, 1b	4:45	10.5	16.9	1230	375	1329	405
2	2a, 2b, 2c, 3a, 3b	6:45	13.5	21.7	1742	531	1247	380
3	3c, 3d, 4a, 4b	8:15	15.8	25.5	1942	592	1988	606
4	5, 6	8:45	16.2	26.1	2051	625	2592	790
5	7a, 7b, 7c, 7d	7:00	14.2	22.8	2097	639	2090	637
6	8a, 8b, 9a	7:30	14.9	23.9	1529	466	1266	386
7	9b, 9c, 9d, 10	8:15	16.5	26.5	1296	395	1768	539

6 Days (N-S)

For fit and experienced hikers who like to move quickly. Day 5 is particularly long.

Day	Stages	Time (hr)	Distance		Ascent		Descent	
			miles	km	ft	m	ft	m
1	1a, 1b, 2a, 2b	7:15	15.8	25.4	1814	553	1900	579
2	2c, 3a, 3b, 3c, 3d	6:30	12.7	20.5	1657	505	1289	393
3	4a, 4b, 5	9:30	18.1	29.1	2369	722	2615	797
4	6, 7a, 7b	8:30	16.1	25.9	2208	673	2461	750
5	7c, 7d, 8a, 8b	10:15	20.3	32.6	2307	703	2156	657
6	9a, 9b, 9c, 9d, 10	9:15	18.6	29.9	1532	467	1860	567

5 Days (N-S)

A very tough itinerary for fit and experienced walkers and runners. Every day is extremely long. The times are based on walking speeds (to enable accurate comparison with the other itineraries) so runners will need to adjust them accordingly.

Day	Stages	Time (hr)	Distance		Ascent		Descent	
			miles	km	ft	m	ft	m
1	1a, 1b, 2a, 2b, 2c	8:15	18.0	29.0	1919	585	2083	635
2	3a, 3b, 3c, 3d, 4a	9:15	17.4	28.0	2585	788	2156	657
3	4b, 5, 6	11:00	20.6	33.2	2461	750	2917	889
4	7a, 7b, 7c, 7d, 8a	11:00	21.6	34.8	3022	921	2674	815
5	8b, 9a, 9b, 9c, 9d, 10	11:45	23.9	38.4	1900	579	2451	747

4 Days (N-S)

A very demanding itinerary for experienced long-distance runners. Day 4 is absolutely brutal. The times are based on walking speeds (to enable accurate comparison with the other itineraries) so runners will need to adjust them accordingly.

Day	Stages	Time (hr)	Distance		Ascent		Descent	
			miles	km	ft	m	ft	m
1	1a, 1b, 2a, 2b, 2c, 3a, 3b	11:30	24.0	38.6	2973	906	2576	785
2	3c, 3d, 4a, 4b, 5	11:45	22.6	36.4	2868	874	3229	984
3	6, 7a, 7b, 7c, 7d	12:15	23.6	38.0	3222	982	3442	1049
4	8a, 8b, 9a, 9b, 9c, 9d, 10	15:45	31.3	50.4	2825	861	3035	925

The Stroudwater Canal (Selsley Variant)

Suggested Itineraries: South to North

12 Days (S-N)

Our most leisurely itinerary is perfect for those who want to relax and take their time. Day 11 of the 11-day itinerary is split in two, enabling you to stay at both Broadway and Stanton. Although your final two days of walking are very short, you will have plenty of spare time to soak up the atmosphere in these exceptional villages. You will also arrive in the wonderful Chipping Campden early on your last day, allowing plenty of time for exploration.

Day	Stages	Time (hr)	Distance		Ascent		Descent	
			miles	km	ft	m	ft	m
1	10	5:30	10.1	16.2	1398	426	787	240
2	9d, 9c, 9b, 9a	4:00	8.5	13.7	463	141	745	227
3	8b, 8a	6:30	12.7	20.5	1175	358	1293	394
4	7d, 7c	3:45	7.5	12.1	981	299	1014	309
5	7b, 7a	3:30	6.7	10.7	1109	338	1083	330
6	6	5:30	9.4	15.2	1352	412	1125	343
7	5	3:45	6.8	10.9	1240	378	925	282
8	4b, 4a	6:00	11.3	18.2	1375	419	1444	440
9	3d, 3c, 3b, 3a	5:00	10.5	16.9	1106	337	1552	473
10	2c, 2b, 2a	3:30	7.5	12.1	755	230	689	210
11	1b	2:00	4.5	7.3	627	191	692	211
12	1a	2:45	6.0	9.6	702	214	538	164

11 Days (S-N)

Day 4 of the standard 10-day itinerary is split into two days with an overnight stop in Dursley.

Day	Stages	Time (hr)	Distance		Ascent		Descent	
			miles	km	ft	m	ft	m
1	10	5:30	10.1	16.2	1398	426	787	240
2	9d, 9c, 9b, 9a	4:00	8.5	13.7	463	141	745	227
3	8b, 8a	6:30	12.7	20.5	1175	358	1293	394
4	7d, 7c	3:45	7.5	12.1	981	299	1014	309
5	7b, 7a	3:30	6.7	10.7	1109	338	1083	330
6	6	5:30	9.4	15.2	1352	412	1125	343
7	5	3:45	6.8	10.9	1240	378	925	282
8	4b, 4a	6:00	11.3	18.2	1375	419	1444	440
9	3d, 3c, 3b, 3a	5:00	10.5	16.9	1106	337	1552	473
10	2c, 2b, 2a	3:30	7.5	12.1	755	230	689	210
11	1b, 1a	4:45	10.5	16.9	1329	405	1230	375

10 Days (S-N)

Our standard schedule which is popular with many walkers because the nightly stops are at some of the loveliest places on the CW (usually with a pub or two and a variety of places to stay). The first day is long but you cannot avoid this as there is no accommodation mid-stage.

Day	Stages	Time (hr)	Distance		Ascent		Descent	
			miles	km	ft	m	ft	m
1	10	5:30	10.1	16.2	1398	426	787	240
2	9d, 9c, 9b, 9a	4:00	8.5	13.7	463	141	745	227
3	8b, 8a	6:30	12.7	20.5	1175	358	1293	394
4	7d, 7c, 7b, 7a	7:15	14.2	22.8	2090	637	2097	639
5	6	5:30	9.4	15.2	1352	412	1125	343
6	5	3:45	6.8	10.9	1240	378	925	282
7	4b, 4a	6:00	11.3	18.2	1375	419	1444	440
8	3d, 3c, 3b, 3a	5:00	10.5	16.9	1106	337	1552	473
9	2c, 2b, 2a	3:30	7.5	12.1	755	230	689	210
10	1b, 1a	4:45	10.5	16.9	1329	405	1230	375

9 Days (S-N)

Days 6 to 9 of the standard 10-day itinerary are squeezed into three days. It is a well-balanced itinerary.

Day	Stages	Time (hr)	Distance		Ascent		Descent	
			miles	km	ft	m	ft	m
1	10	5:30	10.1	16.2	1398	426	787	240
2	9d, 9c, 9b, 9a	4:00	8.5	13.7	463	141	745	227
3	8b, 8a	6:30	12.7	20.5	1175	358	1293	394
4	7d, 7c, 7b, 7a	7:15	14.2	22.8	2090	637	2097	639
5	6	5:30	9.4	15.2	1352	412	1125	343
6	5, 4b	6:00	11.2	18.0	1565	477	1335	407
7	4a, 3d, 3c	6:00	11.4	18.4	1663	507	1532	467
8	3b, 3a, 2c, 2b, 2a	6:15	13.5	21.7	1247	380	1742	531
9	1b, 1a	4:45	10.5	16.9	1329	405	1230	375

8 Days (S-N)

Days 5 to 9 of the 9-day itinerary are squeezed into four days. Unfortunately, the spacing of the accommodation makes it difficult to break the northbound route into eight days of an even length. Day 5 is very long.

Day	Stages	Time (hr)	Distance		Ascent		Descent	
			miles	km	ft	m	ft	m
1	10	5:30	10.1	16.2	1398	426	787	240
2	9d, 9c, 9b, 9a	4:00	8.5	13.7	463	141	745	227
3	8b, 8a	6:30	12.7	20.5	1175	358	1293	394
4	7d, 7c, 7b, 7a	7:15	14.2	22.8	2090	637	2097	639
5	6, 5	9:15	16.2	26.1	2592	790	2051	625
6	4b, 4a	6:00	11.3	18.2	1375	419	1444	440
7	3d, 3c, 3b, 3a, 2c	6:00	12.7	20.5	1289	393	1657	505
8	2b, 2a, 1b, 1a	7:15	15.8	25.4	1900	579	1814	553

7 Days (S-N)

For fit hikers. Days 4 and 5 are very long and hard. Fortunately, the previous three days provide a sensible warm-up by gradually increasing the level of difficulty.

Day	Stages	Time (hr)	Distance		Ascent		Descent	
			miles	km	ft	m	ft	m
1	10, 9d	5:45	10.5	16.9	1463	446	902	275
2	9c, 9b, 9a, 8b	6:30	13.4	21.5	988	301	997	304
3	8a, 7d, 7c	7:30	15.0	24.1	1565	477	1939	591
4	7b, 7a, 6	9:00	16.1	25.9	2461	750	2208	673
5	5, 4b, 4a	9:45	18.1	29.1	2615	797	2369	722
6	3d, 3c, 3b, 3a, 2c	6:00	12.7	20.5	1289	393	1657	505
7	2b, 2a, 1b, 1a	7:15	15.8	25.4	1900	579	1814	553

6 Days (S-N)

For very fit and experienced hikers. The final day is very long and unfortunately, rushes you through some of the most beautiful Cotswold villages.

Day	Stages	Time (hr)	Distance		Ascent		Descent	
			miles	km	ft	m	ft	m
1	10, 9d, 9c	7:15	13.5	21.7	1729	527	1165	355
2	9b, 9a, 8b, 8a	8:45	17.8	28.7	1306	398	1660	506
3	7d, 7c, 7b, 7a	7:15	14.2	22.8	2090	637	2097	639
4	6, 5	9:15	16.2	26.1	2592	790	2051	625
5	4b, 4a, 3d, 3c, 3b	8:45	17.1	27.5	2015	614	2244	684
6	3a, 2c, 2b, 2a, 1b, 1a	10:30	22.7	36.6	2549	777	2671	814

5 Days (S-N)

A tough itinerary for fit and experienced walkers and runners. The times are based on walking speeds (to enable accurate comparison with the other itineraries) so runners will need to adjust them accordingly.

Day	Stages	Time (hr)	Distance		Ascent		Descent	
			miles	km	ft	m	ft	m
1	10, 9d, 9c, 9b, 9a	9:30	18.6	29.9	1860	567	1532	467
2	8b, 8a, 7d, 7c	10:15	20.3	32.6	2156	657	2307	703
3	7b, 7a, 6	9:00	16.1	25.9	2461	750	2208	673
4	5, 4b, 4a, 3d, 3c	12:00	22.6	36.4	3229	984	2868	874
5	3b, 3a, 2c, 2b, 2a, 1b, 1a	11:00	24.0	38.6	2576	785	2973	906

4 Days (S-N)

A very demanding itinerary for experienced long-distance runners. The times are based on walking speeds (to enable accurate comparison with the other itineraries) so runners will need to adjust them accordingly.

Day	Stages	Time (hr)	Distance		Ascent		Descent	
			miles	km	ft	m	ft	m
1	10, 9d, 9c, 9b, 9a, 8b	12:15	23.9	38.4	2451	747	1900	579
2	8a, 7d, 7c, 7b, 7a	11:00	21.6	34.8	2674	815	3022	921
3	6, 5, 4b, 4a	15:15	27.5	44.3	3967	1209	3494	1065
4	3d, 3c, 3b, 3a, 2c, 2b, 2a, 1b, 1a	13:15	28.5	45.9	3189	972	3471	1058

Spring wild-flowers near Haresfield Beacon (Stage 6)

Accommodation

Chipping Campden town centre (Stage 1a)

The CW is a popular trek and there is a wide range of accommodation: 'bed and breakfasts', pubs, hotels and a few hostels. All accommodation is numbered and marked on the OS maps in this book. Detailed accommodation listings are provided on pages 24 to 32. All contact details were correct at the date of press but this information frequently changes. Please let us know about any changes you notice. For camping, see page 23.

Although there is plenty of accommodation along the trail itself, it tends to book up very quickly. As you move further away from the trail, bookings are often easier to secure. In the accommodation listings, any off-route accommodation is labelled 'OR' and we specify its distance from the trail. Bear in mind that the extra time and distance required to travel to, and from, OR accommodation is excluded from the statistics for each stage in the Itinerary Planner: if you intend to stay OR, you will need to allow for this extra time and effort when planning.

These days, most people book the accommodation for their entire trip before they depart. The rise in the number of companies offering unguided trips means that an increasing number of beds are block-booked months in advance. This makes it harder for the independent trekker to secure some of the best locations unless you book well in advance or you are prepared to camp.

In July/August and during other public holidays, the trail is very busy and forward booking is normally essential. You might get lucky and be able to cobble together a set of bookings at the last minute but you are unlikely to get 'first-choice' accommodation right next to the trail.

21

Even outside of July/August, it is wise to book ahead, particularly at weekends and on stages where there is only one place to stay. That said, in April, May, June, September and October, it is still perfectly possible for the independent trekker to secure last-minute bookings, particularly if you are flexible with dates and places and are prepared to stay in towns/villages a short distance OR. Some OR B&Bs may be willing to pick you up from the trail and leave you back the next morning: check when booking. Alternatively, there are local taxi businesses which will pick you up: see 'Public transport along the CW'.

In April (excluding Easter) and October, fewer people walk the route so there is less demand for accommodation. Before April, and from November onwards, some accommodation may be closed so check in advance. For more booking tips, see page 32.

Bed & Breakfasts (B&Bs):
these form the back-bone of CW accommodation. Traditionally, they were private homes which offered rooms and breakfast to visitors. Nowadays, however, you find many bigger and more professionally run properties. Bed and breakfast normally cost £35-70 per person sharing a double/twin room. Rates for solo travellers are usually higher because they pay a single occupancy rate. Normally, the ensuite bedrooms are basic but clean and comfortable. 'Full English' breakfast is the norm: a large helping of bacon, sausage, eggs, mushrooms and black pudding. Most do not provide evening meals but the owner should be able to recommend a local pub or restaurant. Most B&Bs have their own websites and many list their rooms on the generic travel booking sites such as expedia.com or booking.com.

Pubs & Inns:
most villages have a pub and many of them offer bed and breakfast accommodation. This normally costs £35-70 per person sharing a double/twin room. Rates for solo travellers are usually higher because they pay a single occupancy rate. Evening meals are usually available and the standard of food these days is fairly high. Many of the pubs serve a selection of local beers: for some, this is a highlight of the CW. Most pubs have their own websites.

Hotels:
the hotels on offer range from basic ones to more luxury properties. Prices vary widely. They all provide 'Full English' breakfasts and most also offer evening meals. Most hotels have their own websites and many list their rooms on the generic travel booking sites such as expedia.com or booking.com.

Hostels:
these offer beds in dormitories and sometimes private rooms. Generally, they will have shared bathrooms, self-catering kitchen facilities and communal areas. Continental breakfast (tea and toast) is sometimes available. Bedding is usually supplied. Like B&Bs, hostels are becoming more upmarket and prices rise along with the quality of the offering. A bed usually costs £20-30 per person. Groups of two or more may find B&Bs to be better value.

Winchcombe (Stage 2c/3a)

Camping

*Colgate Farm Campsite
(Stage 3d/4a)*

Camping is the cheapest way to hike the CW: a pitch each night costs £5-15 per person. It also usually offers more freedom because campsites rarely need to be booked far in advance (except during July/August and public holiday weekends) and you can often adjust your itinerary as you go. However, it is fair to say that the CW does not serve campers particularly well: wild camping is not permitted and there are not very many campsites along the route. Accordingly, those who wish to camp legally every night will have some very long days. Some trekkers do camp wild without any problems by being discreet and pitching up late, however, we cannot condone this. To help campers plan, a list of campsites is set out below: contact details and information on the facilities are provided in the full Accommodation Listings (see pages 24 to 32).

Normally campsites are clean and well-maintained but some (such as Colgate Farm) can be very basic. Showers are normally provided but you may pay a little extra for this luxury. Even if you have booked in advance, it is always sensible to telephone at least a day or two before so the campsite knows when to expect you.

The obvious downside to camping is that you need to carry a lot more gear: tents, sleeping mats, sleeping bags and stoves all add weight to your pack, making the trek more difficult. In the 'Equipment' section, we provide advice on how to lighten your load. However, another solution is to use a baggage transfer service to transfer your heavy bags between campsites (see 'Baggage transfer').

Stage		Campsite
2b/2c	**35**	Hayles Fruit Farm
3d/4a **Ham Hill**	**48**	Colgate Farm
5/6 **Painswick** (0.4 miles OR)	**64**	Painswick Camping & Glamping
7c/7d **North Nibley**	**74**	Nibley Farm Campsite
8b **Little Sodbury** (0.7 miles OR)	**80**	Cotswold Meadow Camping

Accommodation Listings

			Dormitory
			Private Room
			Camping
			Drinks
			Lunch
			Evening Meals
			Breakfast
			Food shop
			WiFi
OR			Off-route

Stage		Name	Facilities	Contact Details
1a Chipping Campden	1	The Volunteer Inn		01386 840688 info@thevolunteerinn.net www.thevolunteerinn.net
1a Chipping Campden	2	Lygon Arms Hotel		01386 840318/01386 840089 www.lygonarms.co.uk
1a Chipping Campden	3	Red Lion Tavern		01386 840760 info@redliontavern.co.uk www.redliontavern.co.uk
1a Chipping Campden	4	Eight Bells Inn		01386 840371 info@eightbellsinn.co.uk www.eightbellsinn.co.uk
1a Chipping Campden	5	Noel Arms Hotel		01386 840317 www.noelarmschippingcampden.com
1a Chipping Campden	6	Woolmarket House		01386 840374 info@woolmarkethouse.com www.woolmarkethouse.com
1a Chipping Campden	7	Bantam Tea Rooms & Guest House		01386 840386 info@bantamtea-rooms.co.uk www.bantamtea-rooms.co.uk
1a Chipping Campden	8	Badgers Hall		01386 840839 badgershall@gmail.com www.badgershall.com
1a Chipping Campden	9	Cotswold House Hotel & Spa		01386 840330 reservations@cotswoldhouse.com www.cotswoldhouse.com
1a Chipping Campden	10	The Kings Hotel		www.the-kings-hotel.igloucestershire.com **Closed at date of press**

Stage		Name	Facilities	Contact Details
1a Chipping Campden	11	Cornerways B&B	🔒 📶 🍴 Airport & station pick-ups	01386 841307 carole@cornerways.info www.cornerways.info
1a Chipping Campden	12	The Old Bakehouse	🔒 📶 🍴	01386 840979
1a Chipping Campden	13	Park Road B&B	🔒 📶 🍴	01386 641723 info@parkroadbandb.co.uk www.parkroadbandb.co.uk
1a Chipping Campden	14	Taplins B&B	🔒 📶 🍴	01386 841028/840927
1a Chipping Campden	15	Cherry Trees	🔒 📶 🍴	01386 840873
1a/1b Broadway	16	East House Luxury B&B	🔒 📶 🍴	01386 853789/07738 290855 enquiries@easthouseuk.com www.easthouseuk.com
1a/1b Broadway	17	The Olive Branch Guest House	🔒 📶 🍴	01386 853440 www.theolivebranch-broadway.com
1a/1b Broadway	18	Hadley House	🔒 📶 🍴	01386 853486
1a/1b Broadway	19	The Lodge	🔒 📶 🍴	01386 852007 info@thelodgebroadway.co.uk www.thelodgebroadway.co.uk
1a/1b Broadway	20	The Lygon Arms	🔒 📶 🍷 🍴 🍔 🍴	01386 852255 reservations@lygonarmshotel.co.uk www.lygonarmshotel.co.uk
1a/1b Broadway	21	Russell's of Broadway	🔒 📶 🍷 🍴 🍔 🍴	01386 853555 info@russellsofbroadway.co.uk www.russellsofbroadway.co.uk
1a/1b Broadway	22	The Broadway Hotel	🔒 📶 🍷 🍴 🍔 🍴	01386 852401 reception@broadway-hotel.co.uk www.broadway-hotel.co.uk
1a/1b Broadway	23	Crown & Trumpet Inn	🔒 📶 🍷 🍴 🍔 🍴	01386 853202/01386 853036 www.crownandtrumpet.co.uk
1a/1b Broadway	24	Abbots Grange	🔒 📶 🍷 🍴	0208 133 8698 rooms@abbotsgrange.com www.abbotsgrange.com
1a/1b Broadway	25	Windrush House	🔒 📶 🍴	01386 853577 info@windrushhouse.com www.windrushhouse.com
1a/1b Broadway	26	Apple Tree B&B	🔒 📶 🍴	01386 853681 stay@appletreebroadway.co.uk www.appletreebroadway.co.uk

Stage		Name	Facilities	Contact Details
1a/1b **Broadway**	**27**	Brook House B&B	🔒🍴 📶 📶 ☕	07901 820198 brookhousebb@googlemail.com www.brookhousebandb.co.uk
1a/1b **Broadway**	**28**	The Old Station House B&B	🔒🍴 📶 📶 ☕	01386 852659/07783 023535 oldstationhousecotswolds@gmail.com www.oldstationhousebroadway.co.uk
1a/1b **Broadway**	**29**	Horse & Hound pub	🔒🍴 📶 🍷 ☕ 🍔 🍴	01386 852287 dianeanddavidt@gmail.com
1b/2a **Stanton**	**30**	Shenberrow Hill B&B	🔒🍴 📶 📶 ☕	01386 584468/07811 381067 angela@shenberrowhill.co.uk
1b/2a **Stanton**	**31**	The Old Post House B&B	🔒🍴 📶 📶 ☕	01386 584398/07887 660798 jo.imeson1@gmail.com theoldposthousebedbreakfaststanton.co.uk
1b/2a **Stanton**	**32**	The Vine B&B	🔒🍴 📶 📶 ☕	01386 584250/01386 584777/ 07824 469472
2a/2b **Wood Stanway**	**33**	Wood Stanway Farmhouse B&B	🔒🍴 📶 📶 ☕	01386 584318 www.woodstanwayfarmhouse.co.uk
2b (0.2 miles OR)	**34**	North Farmcote B&B	🔒🍴 📶 📶 ☕	01242 602304/07792 328274 davideayrs@yahoo.co.uk www.northfarmcote.co.uk
2b/2c	**35**	Hayles Fruit Farm	⛺ 📶 🍷 ☕ 🍔 🍴 🛒	01242 602123 info@haylesfruitfarm.co.uk www.haylesfruitfarm.co.uk
2c (0.6 miles OR)	**36**	Ireley Farm B&B	🔒🍴 📶 📶 ☕	01242 602445 chloe@ireleyfarm.com www.ireleyfarm.com
2c/3a **Winchcombe**	**37**	The Lion Inn	🔒🍴 📶 🍷 ☕ 🍔 🍴	01242 603300 sleep@thelionwinchcombe.co.uk www.thelionwinchcombe.co.uk
2c/3a **Winchcombe**	**38**	The White Hart Inn	🔒🍴 📶 🍷 ☕ 🍔 🍴	01242 602359 info@whitehartwinchcombe.co.uk www.whitehartwinchcombe.co.uk
2c/3a **Winchcombe**	**39**	Blair House B&B	🔒🍴 📶 📶 ☕	01242 603626 info@blairhousewinchcombe.co.uk www.blairhousewinchcombe.co.uk
2c/3a **Winchcombe**	**40**	The Plaisterers Arms	🔒🍴 📶 🍷 ☕ 🍔 🍴	01242 602358 plaisterers.arms@btinternet.com www.theplaisterersarms.com
2c/3a **Winchcombe**	**41**	Wesley House	🔒🍴 📶 🍷 ☕ 🍔 🍴	01242 602366 enquiries@wesleyhouse.co.uk www.wesleyhouse.co.uk

Stage		Name	Facilities	Contact Details
3a/3b Postlip	42	Postlip Hall Farm B&B	🔑 📶 🍳	01242 603351 valerie-albutt@btconnect.com www.cotswoldsfarmstay.co.uk
3a/3b Postlip	43	The Paddocks Farmhouse B&B	🔑 📶 🍳	01242 603503 dawnalbutt@btinternet.com www.postlip.co.uk
3b/3c Cleeve Hill (0.3 miles OR)	44	Cleeve Hill Hotel	🔑 📶 🍷 🍳	01242 672052 post@cleevehillhotel.co.uk www.cleevehillhotel.co.uk
3b/3c Cleeve Hill (0.3 miles OR)	45	Malvern View B&B	🔑 📶 🍳 Sometimes 2-night minimum stay	01242 672017 info@malvernview.com www.malvernview.com
3b/3c Cleeve Hill (0.3 miles OR)	46	Rising Sun pub	🔑 📶 🍷 🍳 🍺 🍴	01242 676281 www.greeneking-pubs.co.uk
3c/3d (0.5 miles OR)	47	Upper Hill Farm B&B	🔑 📶 🍳	01242 235128/07825 396449 stay@upperhillfarm.co.uk www.upperhillfarm.co.uk
3d/4a Ham Hill	48	Colgate Farm	⛺ 🔑 📶 Cook your own breakfast: food provided	07980 607867 www.colgatefarm.co.uk
3d/4a Ham Hill (1.5 miles OR)	49	The Coachhouse at Glenfall House	🔑 🍳	enquiries@glenfallhouse.co.uk www.coachhouse.glenfallhouse.co.uk
3d/4a Whittington (1.5 miles OR)	50	Whittington Lodge Farm B&B	🔑 📶 🍳 Transport to local pub for dinner	01242 820603/07976 691589 info@whittingtonlodgefarm.com www.whittingtonlodgefarm.com
3d/4a Charlton Kings (1.5 miles OR)	51	Detmore House	🔑 📶 🍳	01242 582868 gillkilminster@btconnect.com www.detmorehouse.com
3d/4a Charlton Kings (1.9 miles OR)	52	The London Inn	🔑 📶 🍷 🍳 🍔 🍴	01242 525606 info@londoninncharltonkings.co.uk www.londoninncharltonkings.uk
4a/4b	53	Star Glamping	🔑 📶 🍷 🍳 🍔 **Breakfast hampers and BBQ packs available**	01242 527631 enquiries@nationalstar.org www.nationalstar.org

Stage		Name	Facilities	Contact Details
4b/5 Birdlip	54	Royal George Hotel	🔒📶🍷 🥐🍔🍴	01452 862506 www.greeneking-pubs.co.uk
5 Little Witcombe (1.5 miles OR)	55	Premier Inn Gloucester (Little Witcombe)	🔒📶🍷 🥐🍔🍴	0333 003 1676 www.premierinn.com
5 Little Witcombe (1.7 miles OR)	56	Cheltenham Chase	🔒📶🍷 🥐🍴	01452 519988 www.thecheltenhamchase.co.uk
5/6 Painswick	57	St Anne's B&B	🔒📶🥐	01452 812879/07774 550427 iris@st-annes-painswick.co.uk www.st-annes-painswick.co.uk
5/6 Painswick	58	Troy House	🔒📶🥐	01452 812339 troyhouse@outlook.com www.troyguesthouse.co.uk
5/6 Painswick	59	Tibbiwell Lodge	🔒📶🥐	01452 812748/07872 310393 lovell_richard@hotmail.com www.tibbiwelllodge.com
5/6 Painswick	60	St Michael's	🔒📶🍷 🥐🍔🍴	01452 812 12 hello@stmichaelsbistro.co.uk www.stmichaelsbistro.co.uk
5/6 Painswick	61	The Falcon	🔒📶🍷 🥐🍴	01452 222820 www.thefalconpainswick.com
5/6 Painswick	62	The Painswick	🔒📶🍷 🥐🍔🍴	01452 813688 enquiries@thepainswick.co.uk www.thepainswick.co.uk
5/6 Painswick	63	Court House Manor B&B	🔒📶🥐 🍷🍴	01452 814849 www.courthousemanor.co.uk
5/6 Painswick (0.4 miles OR)	64	Painswick Camping & Glamping	⛺🔒	07866 520636 info@painswickglamping.co.uk www.painswickglamping.co.uk
6 Kings Stanley (0.4 miles OR)	65	Orchardene B&B	🔒📶🥐	01453 822684 info@orchardene.co.uk www.orchardene.co.uk
6 Kings Stanley (0.5 miles OR)	66	The Grey Cottage B&B	🔒📶🥐	01453 822515 rosemary.reeves@btopenworld.com www.grey-cottage.co.uk
6 Leonard Stanley (0.9 miles OR)	67	The White Hart pub	🔒📶🍷 🥐🍴	01453 451369 whitehartbandb@gmail.com www.whitehartleonardstanley.com
6/7a Middleyard	68	Valley Views B&B	🔒📶🥐	01453 827 458 enquiries@valley-views.com www.valley-views.com

Stage		Name	Facilities	Contact Details
Selsley Variant	69	The Bell Inn	⚿ 🛜 🍷 🥐 🍔 🍴	01453 753801 info@thebellinnselsley.com www.thebellinnselsley.com
7a/7b Uley (0.6 miles OR)	70	The Old Crown Inn	⚿ 🛜 🍷 🥐 🍔 🍴	01453 860502
7b/7c Dursley	71	Woodland House B&B	⚿ 🛜 🥐	01453 298773/07815 060499 woodlandhousebnb@gmail.com www.woodlandhousebnb.co.uk
7b/7c Dursley	72	Ye Olde Dursley Hotel	⚿ 🛜 🍷 🥐 🍔 🍴	01453 542821 www.ye-olde-dursley-hotel.business.site
7c/7d North Nibley	73	Black Horse Inn	⚿ 🛜 🍷 🥐 🍔 🍴	01453 543777 contact@blackhorse-northnibley.co.uk www.blackhorse-northnibley.co.uk
7c/7d North Nibley	74	Nibley Farm Campsite	⛺	07831 696426/01453 543108 At date of press, Nibley House had been sold and it was not clear whether the campsite would re-open
7c/7d North Nibley (0.3 miles OR)	75	Hunt's Court Huts	⚿	01453 544632 contact@huntscourthuts.co.uk www.huntscourthuts.co.uk
7c/7d North Nibley (0.4 miles OR)	76	Forthay B&B	⚿ 🛜 🍷 🥐 🍴	01453 549016 forthaybandb@gmail.com www.forthaybedandbreakfast.co.uk
7d/8a Wotton-under-Edge	77	The Swan Hotel	⚿ 🛜 🍷 🥐 🍔 🍴	01453 843004 info@swanhotelwotton.com www.swanhotelwotton.com
7d/8a Wotton-under-Edge	78	Hawks View B&B	⚿ 🛜 🥐	01453 521441
8a/8b Hawkesbury Upton (0.3 miles OR)	79	The Fox Inn	⚿ 🛜 🍷 🥐 🍔 🍴	01454 238768 thefoxinnhawkesbury@icloud.com www.thefoxinnhawkesbury.com
8b Little Sodbury (0.7 miles OR)	80	Cotswold Meadow Camping	⛺ ⚿	07789 081899 cotswoldmeadowcamping@gmail.com www.cotswoldmeadowcamping.co.uk
8b/9a Old Sodbury	81	The Dog Inn	⚿ 🛜 🍷 🥐 🍔 🍴	01454 312006 thedoginnoldsodbury@gmail.com www.the-dog-inn.co.uk
8b/9a Old Sodbury (0.3 miles OR)	82	Sodbury House	⚿ 🛜 🥐	01454 312847 info@sodburyhouse.co.uk www.sodburyhouse.co.uk
8b/9a Old Sodbury (0.8 miles OR)	83	Cross Hands Hotel	⚿ 🛜 🍷 🥐 🍔 🍴	01454 313000 www.greeneking-pubs.co.uk

Stage		Name	Facilities	Contact Details
8b/9a **Old Sodbury** (1.2 miles OR)	84	Windylands B&B	🔒📶 ☕	01454 323653 jennifer_woolley@hotmail.com www.windylands.co.uk
8b/9a **Old Sodbury**	85	Rock Cottage B&B	🔒📶 📶 ☕	01454 314688
8b/9a **Old Sodbury** (1 miles OR)	86	The Bell Inn	🔒📶 📶 🍷 ☕ 🍔 🍴	01454 325582 www.thebellatoldsodbury.co.uk
9a/9b **Tormarton**	87	The Major's Retreat	🔒📶 🍷 ☕ 🍔 🍴	01454 218263 info@majorsretreat.co.uk www.majorsretreat.co.uk
9a/9b **Tormarton**	88	Compass Inn	🔒📶 📶 🍷 ☕ 🍔 🍴	01454 218242/03330 035245 www.compass-inn.co.uk www.bestwestern.co.uk
9a/9b **Tormarton**	89	Noades House B&B	🔒📶 📶 ☕	01454 218278 www.noadesstudio.co.uk
9b/9c **Tolldown** (0.4 miles OR)	90	The Crown	🔒📶 📶 🍷 ☕ 🍔 🍴	01225 891166 crowntolldown@butcombepubs.com www.butcombe.com
9c/9d **Pennsylvania**	91	Cornflake Cottage B&B	🔒📶 📶 ☕	01225 892592/07999 640049 fairoaks@hotmail.co.uk www.cornflakecottagebandb.co.uk
9c/9d **Pennsylvania**	92	Swan Cottage B&B	🔒📶 📶 ☕ 🍴 Evening meals on request	07831 422994/01225 891419 claire.buhr@gmail.com www.swancottagebandb.co.uk
9d/10 **Cold Ashton** (1 mile OR)	93	Toghill House Farm	🔒📶 📶 ☕	01225 891261 reservation@toghillhousefarm.co.uk www.toghillhousefarm.co.uk
9d/10 **Cold Ashton** (0.6 miles OR)	94	Whiteways B&B	🔒📶 📶 ☕	01225 891333 (At date of press, it was unclear if B&B would open in 2022)
9d/10 **Marshfield** (2.2 miles OR)	95	The Catherine Wheel pub	🔒📶 📶 🍷 ☕ 🍔 🍴	01225 892220 roo@thecatherinewheel.co.uk www.thecatherinewheel.co.uk
10 (On the CW; 1 mile SW of Cold Ashton)	96	Hill Farm B&B	🔒📶 📶 ☕ 🍴	01225 891952 lucy@hillfarmbath.com www.hillfarmbath.com
10 **Lansdown** (0.8 miles OR)	97	The Charlcombe Inn	🔒📶 📶 🍷 ☕ 🍔 🍴	01225 421995 bookings@charlcombeinn.co.uk www.charlcombeinn.co.uk
10 **Bath**	98	YMCA Bath	🔒📶 🛏 📶 ☕ 🍴	01225 325900 stay@ymca-bg.org www.ymcabath.org.uk

Stage		Name	Facilities	Contact Details
10 Bath	99	St Christopher's Inns Hostel	🔒 🛏 📶 🥐	01225 481444 reception.bath@st-christophers.co.uk www.st-christophers.co.uk
10 Bath	100	Bath Backpackers	🛏 📶	01225 446787 bath@hostels.co.uk www.hostels.co.uk
10 Bath	101	Brooks Guesthouse	🔒 📶 🥐	01225 425543 info@brooksguesthouse.com www.brooksguesthouse.com
10 Bath	102	Brocks Guesthouse	🔒 📶 🥐	01225 338374 brocks@brocksguesthouse.co.uk www.brocksguesthouse.co.uk
10 Bath	103	The Belmont B&B	🔒 📶 🥐	01225 423082 stay@belmontbath.co.uk www.belmontbath.co.uk
10 Bath	104	Anabelle's Guest House	🔒 📶 🥐	01225 330133 www.anabellesguesthouse.co.uk
10 Bath	105	The Henry Guest House	🔒 📶 🥐	01225 424052 stay@thehenry.com www.thehenry.com
10 Bath	106	Eight Hotel	🔒 📶 🍷 🥐 🍴	01225 724111 info@eightinbath.co.uk www.eightinbath.co.uk
10 Bath	107	Rising Sun Inn	🔒 📶 🍷 🥐 🍔 🍴	01225 425918 therisingsunbath@gmail.com www.therisingsunbath.co.uk
10 Bath	108	Premier Inn Bath City Centre	🔒 📶 🍷 🥐 🍴	0333 321 9326 www.premierinn.com
10 Bath	109	Travelodge Bath City Centre	🔒 📶 🥐	08719 846523 www.travelodge.co.uk
10 Bath	110	The Z Hotel	🔒 📶 🥐	01225 613160 bath@thezhotels.com www.thezhotels.com
10 Bath	111	The Gainsborough Bath Spa	🔒 📶 🍷 🥐 🍔 🍴	01225 358888 reservations@ thegainsboroughbathspa.co.uk www.thegainsboroughbathspa.co.uk
10 Bath	112	Harington's Hotel	🔒 📶 🍷 🥐 🍔	01225 461728 post@haringtonshotel.co.uk www.haringtonshotel.co.uk
10 Bath	113	DoubleTree by Hilton	🔒 📶 🍷 🥐 🍔 🍴	www.hilton.com
10 Bath	114	Queensberry Hotel	🔒 📶 🍷 🥐 🍔 🍴	01225 447928 reservations@thequeensberry.co.uk www.thequeensberry.co.uk

Stage		Name	Facilities	Contact Details
10 Bath	115	The Black Fox pub	🛏🍴📶🍷 🍵🍔🍴	01225 442365 info@blackfoxbath.com www.blackfoxbath.com
10 Bath	116	Apex City of Bath Hotel	🛏🍴📶🍷 🍵🍔🍴	0800 049 8000 www.apexhotels.co.uk
10 Bath	117	The Bath House B&B	🛏🍴📶 🍵	07711 119847/01179 374495 info@thebathhouse.org www.thebathhouse.org
10 Bath	118	Broad Street Townhouse Hotel	🛏🍴📶🍷 🍵🍔🍴	01225 330190 reception.broadstreettownhouse@ butcombepubs.com www.butcombe.com
10 Bath	119	Francis Hotel Bath	🛏🍴📶🍷 🍵🍔🍴	01225 424105 h6636@accor.com www.all.accor.com
10 Bath	120	Hotel Indigo Bath	🛏🍴📶🍷 🍵🍔🍴	01225 460441 www.bath.hotelindigo.com

Booking Tips

► The CW becomes more popular each year. To ensure that you secure your accommodation of choice, book as early as you can. Many trekkers start booking in autumn (just after the current summer season has ended) for the following season.

► Try to book 'hot-spots' first: generally, these are places where there are only a few accommodation options. Once you have secured the accommodation which books up most quickly, you can normally slot in the rest of your accommodation more easily. If you leave hot-spots until last then you might have to unwind and rebook other reservations if any hot-spots that you desire are unavailable.

► Start mid-week. A large number of trekkers start the trail at the weekend. Those who start mid-week are often 'out of sync' with the bulk of the trekkers and may therefore find accommodation more easily.

► Weekends are normally busier (even in low season).

► If you cannot get accommodation along the CW itself, try looking for beds in towns/villages a few miles away.

► Those who hike alone, or in pairs, will find it easiest to find beds. For larger groups, it is more difficult.

► If you cannot secure the accommodation that you need then contact one of the unguided tour companies or accommodation booking services. They block-book accommodation months in advance and may have spaces.

► Occasionally, the last-minute booker can get lucky: tour companies which pre-book in blocks will release unsold beds a few weeks or months before the relevant dates. If you call a few weeks before your trip, you may be lucky enough to bag some beds which have just been released.

Facilities

Stage	Place	Dormitory Beds	Private Rooms	Camping	Meals/Drinks	Food Shop	Transport
1a	Chipping Campden		♦		🍴🥤🍺	🧺	🚌
1a/1b	Broadway		♦		🍴🥤🍺	🧺	🚌🚆
1b/2a	Stanton		♦		🍴🥤🍺		🚌🚆
2a (0.9 miles OR)	Toddington						🚆
2a/2b	Wood Stanway		♦				
2b/2c	Hayles Fruit Farm			⌄			
2c	Hailes Abbey					🧺	🚆
2c/3a	Winchcombe		♦		🍴🥤🍺	🧺	🚌🚆
3a/3b	Postlip		♦				🚌
3b/3c	Cleeve Hill		♦		🍴🍺		🚌
3c/3d	Upper Hill Farm exit		♦				
3d/4a	Ham Hill		♦	⌄			
3d/4a (1.5-1.9 miles OR)	Charlton Kings		♦		🍴🥤🍺	🧺	🚌

33

Stage	Place	Dormitory Beds	Private Rooms	Camping	Meals/Drinks	Food Shop	Transport
3c/3d/4a (3.5 miles OR)	Cheltenham		✓		✓	✓	🚆 🚌
4a	Seven Springs				✓		🚌
4a/4b	Ullenwood		✓		✓		🚌
4b/5	Birdlip		✓		✓		🚌
5 (1.5 miles OR)	Little Witcombe		✓		✓		
5/6	Painswick		✓	▲ OR	✓	✓	🚌 🚆
6 (0.6 miles OR)	Stonehouse				✓		🚌
6 (0.4 miles OR)	Kings Stanley		✓		✓	✓	🚌
6/7a	Middleyard		✓				🚌
Selsley Variant	Ebley				✓		🚌
Selsley Variant (1.7 miles OR)	Stroud		✓		✓	✓	🚆 🚌
Selsley Variant	Selsley		✓		✓		🚌

Stage	Place	Dormitory Beds	Private Rooms	Camping	Meals/Drinks	Food Shop	Transport
7a/7b (0.6 miles OR)	Uley		🛏		🍷 🍴	🛒	🚌
7b/7c	Dursley		🛏		🍷 🍴	🛒	🚌 🚌
7c/7d	North Nibley		🛏	⛺	🍷 🍴		
7d/8a	Wotton-under-Edge		🛏		🍷 🍴	🛒	🚌
8a	Alderley				🍴		🚌
8a/8b	Hawkesbury Upton		🛏		🍷 🍴	🛒	🚌
8b	Horton						🚌
8b/9a	Old Sodbury		🛏	⛺ OR	🍷 🍴		🚌
9a/9b	Tormarton		🛏		🍷 🍴		
9b/9c (0.4 miles OR)	Tolldown		🛏		🍷 🍴		
9c/9d	Pennsylvania		🛏 OR		🍴 🍷 OR	🛒	
9d/10	Cold Ashton		🛏		🍷 🍴		🚌
10	Weston		🛏		🍷 🍴	🛒	🚌
10	Bath	🛏			🍷 🍴	🛒	🚌 🚌

Food

The shop at Hayles Fruit Farm (Stage 2b/2c)

Breakfast: for most trekkers, breakfast will be provided as part of the overnight package at B&Bs, pubs or hotels. Normally, this will be a 'Full English' breakfast which is a large helping of bacon, sausage, eggs, mushrooms and black pudding.

Lunch: most accommodation providers can prepare a packed lunch for you. Be sure to request this the night before. Alternatively, on some stages, you can stop for lunch at a pub or café along the route. Pubs/cafés located mid-stage are marked on the maps: unfortunately, at overnight stops, there are too many pubs/cafés to mark them on the maps.

Evening meals: if your accommodation does not offer evening meals then the staff will usually be able to recommend a pub or restaurant within walking distance. Most villages have a pub/inn, serving food and excellent beer. In fact, for many trekkers, the 'pub grub' and 'real ale' are highlights of the CW: the beers available are some of England's finest.

Self-catering: there are many grocery shops and small supermarkets that serve the CW and they are listed in the route descriptions. Some of the shops are in towns and villages which the trail actually passes through. However, other shops are a short distance OR. Often the shops are small with a limited range of products but, as long as you are not too fussy, you should find plenty to eat. However, if you are more particular, or you have specific nutritional requirements, you may wish to stock up on supplies before setting out on the trek.

However, remember that food is heavy so, unless you are travelling very quickly, you may not be able to start the trek with all the food that you will require for the full distance. It is much better to accept at the outset that you can only carry a few days' food than to exhaust yourself in the early stages of the trek by carrying too much. Many campers carry only a small amount of food which they supplement with meals at pubs and cafés along the way. It is sensible to carry dried food (such as pasta and rice): water is food's heaviest component. Pre-packed freeze-dried meals for backpackers are an excellent choice because they are light and are prepared simply by adding boiling water.

Travel

Beautiful views from the Cotswold Escarpment (Stage 4a)

Travel to England

There are numerous airports in the UK and, in normal times, there are plenty of domestic and international flights available. At the date of press, however, many services were not operating due to COVID-19 and it was not clear if, or when, they would resume.

Bristol is the most convenient airport for Bath (the S trail-head). There are flights to Bristol Airport from a variety of cities in the UK, Ireland and mainland Europe. Bath is only 55min away from the airport by bus (hourly; www.airdecker.com) or you could take a taxi (£65; Arrow Cars; www.arrowcars.co.uk). To get from Bristol Airport to Chipping Campden (the N trail-head), first travel to Bristol by taxi or the Airport Flyer bus (every 20-30min; www.firstbus.co.uk): then take a train to Cheltenham from Bristol Temple Meads Station or go by bus from Bristol Bus Station (daily; 1-1.25hr; www.nationalexpress.com). For travel from Cheltenham to Chipping Campden, see 'Travel to/from the primary trail-heads'.

Birmingham has the closest airport to the N trail-head and there are flights to/from a variety of cities in the UK, Ireland and mainland Europe. Birmingham International Station is located at the airport and there are trains to a number of towns close to Chipping Campden including Moreton-in-Marsh (2hr), Evesham (1.75hr), Cheltenham (1.25hr) and Stratford-upon-Avon (1.5hr), although in each case you will have to change trains: for travel from these places to Chipping Campden, see 'Travel to/from the primary trail-heads'. You can also get a taxi from Birmingham Airport to Chipping Campden which is cost effective in a group (1hr; £60; www.uber.com): it is cheaper and easier to get picked up from the airport's train station rather than the airport terminal itself. There are also trains between Birmingham Airport and Bath (2.5hr).

Further away are the various **London** airports (London City, London Luton, London Heathrow, London Stansted and London Gatwick). From each, there are a variety of different travel options to the Cotswolds but often you will first need to travel into the centre of London or another English city.

Travel to/from the primary trail-heads

Those walking N-S will start from Chipping Campden. Those walking S-N will start from Bath. For travel from nearby airports to Bath or Chipping Campden, see 'Travel to England'.

By train: to check train times and buy tickets, see **www.thetrainline.com**.

▶ **Bath** is well-connected to the rest of GB by rail although, depending upon your departure point, you may have to change a few times.

▶ **Chipping Campden** is not on a train line: the nearest stations are Moreton-in-Marsh (6 miles), Evesham (10 miles), Stratford-upon-Avon (13 miles) and Cheltenham (23 miles). There are buses to Chipping Campden from each of these places (see below), however, services are infrequent so it can be more convenient to take a taxi (see below).

By bus: there are coaches between Bath and London Victoria Coach Station. Coaches also operate to Cheltenham (from Birmingham and London) and Stratford-upon-Avon (from London): onward travel to Chipping Campden would be by local bus or taxi. For further information on coach travel, see www.nationalexpress.com or www.uk.megabus.com. Long-distance coaches within the UK often take longer than trains.

Local bus services to Chipping Campden operate from a variety of places including the following places. For further information, see 'Public transport along the CW'.

► **Moreton-in-Marsh:** Johnsons Coaches 1 & 2 (Mon-Sat)

► **Evesham:** Hedgehog Bus H5A (Tue & Thur only)

► **Stratford-upon-Avon:** Johnsons Coaches 1 & 2 (Mon-Sat); Hedgehog Bus H3A/H3B/H3C/H3E (Tue, Wed, Fri & Sat)

► **Cheltenham:** Pulhams Coaches 606 (Mon-Sat); 608 (Thur)

By car: you could park your car in Chipping Campden or Bath and use public transport to return to it at the end of the trek (see 'Returning to the start'). If you are staying at a hotel/B&B in Chipping Campden or Bath, they may let you park your car long-term for a fee: check when booking. In Chipping Campden, there is free parking on Back Ends near St Catherine's School, however, space is limited: see www.chippingcampdenonline.org. Free parking is harder to find in Bath, however, you can book reasonably priced parking at www.yourparkingspace.co.uk. As an alternative, Carryabag (see 'Baggage transfer') has parking spaces in Cheltenham: if you leave your car there, they can drive you to the start of the CW and then pick you up again at the finish.

By taxi: there are plenty of taxi operators that serve Chipping Campden and Bath including those listed below.

Chipping Campden:

► **Cotswold Premier (Chipping Campden)**: www.cotswoldcartours.co.uk; tim@cotswoldcartours.co.uk; 07873 117445/01386 840927

► **Red Lion Private Hire (Chipping Campden)**: www.redlionprivatehire.co.uk; 07565 226887

► **Northwick Private Hire (Chipping Campden)**: www.cotswold-taxis.com; 01386 701806/07855 824788

► **Claremont Cars (Evesham)**: www.claremontcars.co.uk; 01386 833660

► **Swan Taxis (Stratford-upon-Avon)**: www.swan-taxis.co.uk; enquiries@swan-taxis.co.uk; 01789 750935/07767 126582

Bath:

► **V Cars**: www.v-cars.com; bath@v-cars.com; 01225 464646

► **Bath Taxi Transfers**: www.bathtaxitransfers.co.uk; 01225 220789

► **Russells of Bath**: www.russellsofbath.com; russellsofbath@gmail.com; 01225 683058

► **Bath Private Car Hire**: www.bathprivatecarhire.com; 01225 282101/07900 187257

► **Bath Airport Taxis**: www.bath-airport-taxis.co.uk; 01225 764141

Returning to the start

If you leave a car or luggage at your start point, you can use public transport to return to it at the end of the trek. There are trains between Bath Spa Station and a number of towns near Chipping Campden including Cheltenham (1.25-1.75hr), Evesham (2-2.5hr) and Moreton-in-Marsh (2hr): for onward travel to Chipping Campden, take a bus or taxi (see 'Travel to/from the primary trail-heads'). To check train times and buy tickets, see www.thetrainline.com.

Public transport along the CW

There are numerous bus and train services that are useful to the CW walker. Many stop at places along the CW itself but others serve towns/villages which are a short distance OR. In this book, we refer to all of these places (other than the primary trail-heads at Chipping Campden and Bath) as 'secondary trail-heads' and there is a list of them on pages 43 to 45, together with details of the relevant transport options: these services can be useful if you need to abandon the trek for any reason or if you wish to skip a stage or two. They can also assist if you are only intending to walk part of the CW: see 'Hiking shorter sections of the CW'.

Train: other than the station at Bath, the closest mainline station to the CW itself is at Stonehouse (Stage 6; 0.6 miles OR). However, there are also stations at some towns which are slightly further away from the trail: Cheltenham (Stage 3c/3d/4a; 3.5 miles OR), Cam & Dursley (Stage 7b/7c; 2.8miles OR), Stroud (1.7 miles OR from the Selsley Variant) and Gloucester (Stage 5; 5.7 miles OR). From these stations, you can travel to many destinations including Bath, Birmingham and London. For tickets and timetables, see www.thetrainline.com.

The Gloucestershire Warwickshire Steam Railway is a volunteer operated heritage railway which operates during the main hiking season between Broadway and Cheltenham Racecourse. On the way, it stops at Toddington (Stage 2a; 0.9 miles OR from Stanway), Hailes Abbey (Stage 2c) and Winchcombe (Stage 2c/3a). Travelling by steam train is a wonderful experience. For timetables and further information, see www.gwsr.com.

Buses: the key services operating close to the CW are set out below. There are too many bus services operating in the region to list them all.

Bus Service	Key Information (Places in red have a mainline train station)
Community Connexions 21 (Wed & Fri)	**Birdlip** (Stage 4b/5) - **Gloucester**
Cotswold Green 40 (Mon-Sat)	**Wotton-under-Edge** (Stage 7d/8a) - **Stroud** (Selsley Variant; 1.7 miles OR)
Cotswold Green 65A (Sat)	**Stroud** (Selsley Variant; 1.7 miles OR) - **Selsley** (Selsley Variant) - **Uley** (Stage 7a/7b; 0.6 miles OR) - **Dursley** (Stage 7b/7c)
Euro Taxis 626 (Mon-Fri)	**Wotton-under-Edge** (Stage 7d/8a) - **Bristol**

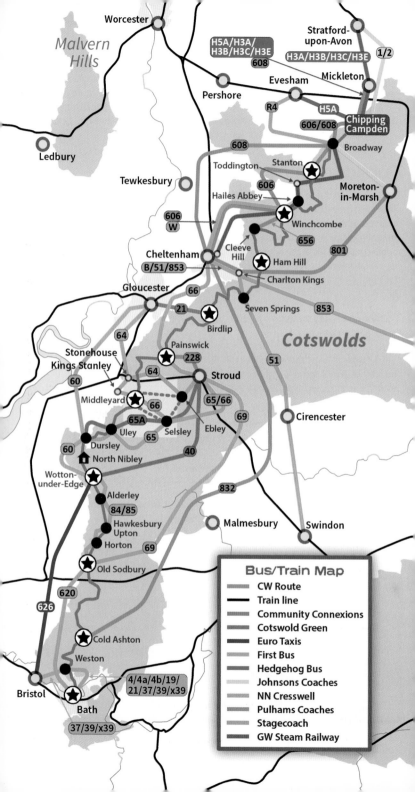

Worcester

Malvern Hills

Stratford-upon-Avon

H5A/H3A/H3B/H3C/H3E 608

H3A/H3B/H3C/H3E 1/2

Mickleton

Pershore

Evesham

R4

H5A

Ledbury

606/608

Chipping Campden

608

Broadway

Tewkesbury

Toddington

Stanton ★

Moreton-in-Marsh

606

Hailes Abbey

606 W

★ Winchcombe

656

Cheltenham

B/51/853

Cleve Hill

Charlton Kings

801

66

Gloucester

★ Ham Hill

Seven Springs

853

64

21

★ Birdlip

Cotswolds

Stonehouse
Kings Stanley

Painswick ★

228

60

64

Stroud

Middleyard ★

66

65/66

Cirencester

65A

51

Uley

65

Selsley

Ebley

69

Dursley

North Nibley

40

60

832

Wotton-under-Edge ★

Malmesbury

Swindon

Alderley

84/85

Hawkesbury Upton

Horton

69

Old Sodbury ★

620

626

Cold Ashton ★

Weston

4/4a/4b/19/21/37/39/x39

Bristol

★ Bath

37/39/x39

Bus/Train Map

- CW Route
- Train line
- Community Connexions
- Cotswold Green
- Euro Taxis
- First Bus
- Hedgehog Bus
- Johnsons Coaches
- NN Cresswell
- Pulhams Coaches
- Stagecoach
- GW Steam Railway

Bus Service	Key Information (Places in red have a mainline train station)
First Bus 4/4a/4b/19/21 (Daily)	**Weston** (Stage 10) - Bath **Bus Station** (Stage 10)
First Bus 37/39/x39 (Daily)	Bristol **Bus Station** - **Weston** (Stage 10) - Bath **Bus Station** (Stage 10)
Hedgehog Bus H5A (Tue & Thur)	Evesham - **Chipping Campden** (Stage 1a) - Mickleton
Hedgehog Bus H3A/ H3B/H3C/H3E (Tue, Wed, Fri & Sat)	Stratford-upon-Avon - **Chipping Campden** (Stage 1a) - Mickleton
Johnsons Coaches 1 & 2 (Mon-Sat)	Stratford-upon-Avon - **Chipping Campden** (Stage 1a) - **Broadway** (Stage 1a/1b) - Moreton-in-Marsh
NN Cresswell R4 (Mon-Fri)	**Broadway** (Stage 1a/1b) - Evesham
Pulhams Coaches 228 (Thur)	**Painswick** (Stage 5/6) - Stroud (Selsley Variant; 1.7 miles OR)
Pulhams Coaches 606 (Mon-Sat)	**Chipping Campden** (Stage 1a) - **Broadway** (Stage 1a/1b) - **Stanton** (Stage 1b/2a) - **Winchcombe** (Stage 2c/3a) - Cheltenham
Pulhams Coaches 608 (Thur)	Mickleton - **Chipping Campden (Stage 1a)** - **Broadway (Stage 1a/1b)** - Cheltenham
Pulhams Coaches 656 (Mon-Fri)	**Winchcombe** (Stage 2c/3a) - **Cleeve Hill** (Stage 3b/3c; Rising Sun Hotel)
Pulhams Coaches 801 (Mon-Sat)	Cheltenham - **Charlton Kings** (Stage 3d/4a; OR) - Moreton-in-Marsh
Pulhams Coaches 832 (Wed)	Cheltenham - **Cold Ashton** (Stage 9d/10)
Stagecoach 853 (Daily)	Cheltenham - **Charlton Kings** (Stage 3d/4a; OR) - Oxford
Stagecoach W (Mon-Fri)	Cheltenham - **Winchcombe** (Stage 2c/3a)
Stagecoach B (Daily)	Cheltenham - **Charlton Kings** (Stage 3d/4a; OR)
Stagecoach 51 (Daily)	Cheltenham - **Charlton Kings** (Stage 3d/4a; OR) - **Seven Springs** (Stage 4a) - **Cirencester** - Swindon
Stagecoach 60 (Daily)	**Wotton-under-Edge** (Stage 7d/8a) - **Dursley** (Stage 7b/7c) - Gloucester
Stagecoach 64 (Daily)	Stroud (Selsley Variant; 1.7 miles OR) - **Ebley** (Selsley Variant) **Stonehouse** (Stage 6; 0.6 miles OR) - Gloucester
Stagecoach 65 (Mon-Fri)	Stroud (Selsley Variant; 1.7 miles OR) - **Selsley** (Selsley Variant) - **Uley** (Stage 7a/7b; 0.6 miles OR) - **Dursley** (Stage 7b/7c)
Stagecoach 66 (Daily)	Cheltenham - **Painswick** (Stage 5/6) - Stroud (Selsley Variant; 1.7 miles OR) - **Selsley** (Selsley Variant) - **Middleyard** (Stage 6/7a) - **Kings Stanley** (Stage 6; 0.4 miles OR) - **Stonehouse** (Stage 6; 0.6 miles OR)

Bus Service	Key Information (Places in red have a mainline train station)
Stagecoach 69 (Mon-Sat)	**Old Sodbury** (Stage 8b/9a) - **Stroud** (Selsley Variant; 1.7 miles OR)
Stagecoach 84/85 (Mon-Sat)	**Wotton-under-Edge** (Stage 7d/8a) - **Alderley** (Stage 8a) **Hawkesbury Upton** (Stage 8a/8b) - **Horton** (Stage 8b) - **Old Sodbury** (Stage 8b/9a) - **Chipping Sodbury**
Stagecoach 620 (Mon-Sat)	**Old Sodbury** (Stage 8b/9a) - **Bath** (Stage 10)

Further information about bus travel:

Community Connexions: www.communityconnexions.org.uk

Cotswold Green: 01453 835153; admin@cotswoldgreen.com

Euro Taxis: www.eurotaxis.com

First Bus: www.firstbus.co.uk

Hedgehog Bus: www.hedgehogbus.org

Johnsons Coaches: www.johnsonscoaches.co.uk

NN Cresswell: www.nncresswell.co.uk

Pulhams Coaches: www.pulhamscoaches.com

Stagecoach: www.stagecoachbus.com

Taxis: there are many taxi businesses operating from towns/villages near the CW. They can often pick you up from the CW, drive you to nearby accommodation and leave you back to the CW the next morning. Some of them operate surprisingly far from their hubs. There are too many taxi businesses to list them all but some of the useful services include:

► **Chipping Campden taxi services:** see 'Travel to/from the primary trail-heads'

► **Broadway Taxis (Broadway):** www.broadwaytaxis.co.uk; 07407 707044

► **Cotswold Luxury Transfers (Broadway):** www.cotswoldluxurytransfers.co.uk; 07775 488074

► **Taylor Private Hire (Winchcombe):** 07814 570876

► **P Private Hire (Winchcombe):** www.aprivatehire.wixsite.com; 07845 720562

► **Starline Taxis (Cheltenham):** www.starlinetaxis.com; 01242 250250,

► **Dial-a-cab (Cheltenham):** www.taxicheltenham.co.uk; 01242 242424

► **Stroud Taxis (Stroud):** www.stroudtaxi.co.uk; 01453 750211

► **Apollo Taxis (Stonehouse/Stroud):** www.apollotaxi.co.uk; 01453 823344

► **Cam & Dursley Taxis (Dursley):** www.camanddursleytaxis.co.uk; 07475 313151

► **Dursley Taxis (Dursley):** www.dursleytaxis.co.uk; 07833 264099

► **Hop-In Taxis (Wotton-under-Edge):** www.hop-in-taxis-ltd.business.site; 01453 521444/07968 029724

► **Wotton Executives (Wotton-under-Edge):** www.wottonexecutives.co.uk; 07814 511423/07814 511423

► **Chipping Sodbury Taxis (Chipping Sodbury):** www.chippingsodburytaxis.co.uk; 07891 190984

► **PJ Cabs (Chipping Sodbury):** www.pjcabs.co.uk; 01454 313131

► **Bath taxi services:** see 'Travel to/from the primary trail-heads'

Secondary trail-heads

Secondary Trail-head	Possible Destinations (Mainline train stations in red)	Bus/Train Services
1a Chipping Campden	**Broadway** (Stage 1a/1b) **Stanton** (Stage 1b/2a) **Winchcombe** (Stage 2c/3a) Cheltenham Stratford-upon-Avon Moreton-in-Marsh Evesham Mickleton	**Pulhams Coaches 606** **Johnsons Coaches 1 & 2** **Hedgehog Bus H3A/H3B/H3C/H3E** **Hedgehog Bus H5A** **Pulhams Coaches 608**
1a/1b Broadway	**Chipping Campden** (Stage 1a) **Stanton** (Stage 1b/2a) **Winchcombe** (Stage 2c/3a) Cheltenham Stratford-upon-Avon Moreton-in-Marsh Mickleton Evesham **Toddington/Hailes Abbey**	**Pulhams Coaches 606** **Johnsons Coaches 1 & 2** **Pulhams Coaches 608** **NN Cresswell R4** **GWSR Heritage Railway**
1b/2a Stanton	**Chipping Campden** (Stage 1a) **Broadway** (Stage 1a/1b) **Winchcombe** (Stage 2c/3a) Cheltenham	**Pulhams Coaches 606**
2a Toddington (0.9 miles OR)	**Broadway** (Stage 1a/1b) **Hailes Abbey** (Stage 2c) **Winchcombe** (Stage 2c/3a)	**GWSR Heritage Railway**
2c Hailes Abbey halt (0.5 miles OR)	**Broadway** (Stage 1a/1b) **Toddington** (Stage 2a) **Winchcombe** (Stage 2c/3a)	**GWSR Heritage Railway**
2c/3a Winchcombe	**Chipping Campden** (Stage 1a) **Broadway** (Stage 1a/1b) **Stanton** (Stage 1b/2a) Cheltenham **Cleeve Hill** (Stage 3b/3c)	**Pulhams Coaches 606** **Pulhams Coaches 656** **Stagecoach W** **GWSR Heritage Railway**
3b/3c Cleeve Hill	**Winchcombe** (Stage 2c/3a)	**Pulhams Coaches 656**
3d/4a Charlton Kings (1.5 miles OR)	Cheltenham Moreton-in-Marsh **Seven Springs** (Stage 4a) Cirencester Swindon, Oxford	**Pulhams Coaches 801** **Stagecoach B** **Stagecoach 51** **Stagecoach 853**
4a Seven Springs	Cheltenham **Charlton Kings** (Stage 3d/4a; 1.5 miles OR) Cirencester Swindon	**Stagecoach 51**
4b/5 Birdlip (0.1 miles OR)	Gloucester	**Community Connexions 21**

Secondary Trail-head	Possible Destinations (Mainline train stations in red)	Bus/Train Services
5/6 Painswick	Cheltenham **Stonehouse** (Stage 6; 0.6 miles OR) **Stroud** (Selsley Variant; 1.7 miles OR) **Selsley** (Selsley Variant) **Kings Stanley** (Stage 6; 0.4 miles OR) **Middleyard** (Stage 6/7a)	**Stagecoach 66** **Pulhams Coaches 228**
6 Stonehouse (0.6 miles OR)	**Ebley** (Selsley Variant) **Painswick** (Stage 5/6) **Stroud** (Selsley Variant; 1.7 miles OR) **Selsley** (Selsley Variant) **Middleyard** (Stage 6/7a) **Kings Stanley** (Stage 6; 0.4 miles OR) Cheltenham, Gloucester **Bath/Birmingham/London (by train)**	**Stagecoach 64/66** **Train**
6 Kings Stanley (0.4 miles OR)	Cheltenham **Painswick** (Stage 5/6) **Middleyard** (Stage 6/7a) Stonehouse (Stage 6; 0.6 miles OR) Stroud (Selsley Variant; 1.7 miles OR) **Selsley** (Selsley Variant)	**Stagecoach 66**
6/7a Middleyard	Cheltenham **Painswick** (Stage 5/6) **Kings Stanley** (Stage 6; 0.4 miles OR) **Stonehouse** (Stage 6; 0.6 miles OR) **Stroud** (Selsley Variant; 1.7 miles OR) **Selsley** (Selsley Variant)	**Stagecoach 66**
Ebley Selsley Variant	Stonehouse (Stage 6; 0.6 miles OR) Stroud (Selsley Variant; 1.7 miles OR) Gloucester	**Stagecoach 64**
Stroud (1.7 miles OR) **Selsley Variant**	**Painswick** (Stage 5/6) **Ebley** (Selsley Variant) **Selsley** (Selsley Variant) Stonehouse (Stage 6; 0.6 miles OR) **Middleyard** (Stage 6/7a) **Kings Stanley** (Stage 6; 0.4 miles OR) **Uley** (Stage 7a/7b; 0.6 miles OR) **Dursley** (Stage 7b/7c) **Wotton-under-Edge** (Stage 7d/8a) **Old Sodbury** (Stage 8b/9a) Gloucester Cheltenham **Bath/Birmingham/London (by train)**	**Cotswold Green 40/65A** **Pulhams Coaches 228** **Stagecoach 64/65/66/69** **Train**
Selsley Selsley Variant	**Painswick** (Stage 5/6) Stonehouse (Stage 6; 0.6 miles OR) **Middleyard** (Stage 6/7a) **Kings Stanley** (Stage 6; 0.4 miles OR) Stroud (Selsley Variant; 1.7 miles OR) Uley (Stage 7a/7b; 0.6 miles OR) **Dursley (Stage 7b/7c)** Cheltenham	**Stagecoach 65/66** **Cotswold Green 65A**

Secondary Trail-head	Possible Destinations (Mainline train stations in red)	Bus/Train Services
7a/7b Uley	Stroud (Selsley Variant; 1.7 miles OR) Selsley (Selsley Variant) Dursley (Stage 7b/7c)	Stagecoach 65 Cotswold Green 65A
7b/7c Dursley	Stroud (Selsley Variant; 1.7 miles OR) Selsley (Selsley Variant) Uley (Stage 7a/7b; 0.6 miles OR) Wotton-under-Edge (Stage 7d/8a) Gloucester Bath/Birmingham/London (by train from Cam & Dursley station)	Stagecoach 60 Stagecoach 65 Cotswold Green 65A Train from Cam & Dursley station (2.8 miles OR)
7d/8a Wotton-under-Edge	Stroud (Selsley Variant; 1.7 miles OR) Dursley (Stage 7b/7c) Gloucester Alderley (Stage 8a) Hawkesbury Upton (Stage 8a/8b) Horton (Stage 8b) Old Sodbury (Stage 8b/9a) Chipping Sodbury Bristol	Cotswold Green 40 Stagecoach 60 Stagecoach 84/85 Euro Taxis 626
8a Alderley	Wotton-under-Edge (Stage 7d/8a) Hawkesbury Upton (Stage 8a/8b) Horton (Stage 8b) Old Sodbury (Stage 8b/9a) Chipping Sodbury	Stagecoach 84/85
8a/8b Hawkesbury Upton	Wotton-under-Edge (Stage 7d/8a) Alderley (Stage 8a) Horton (Stage 8b) Old Sodbury (Stage 8b/9a) Chipping Sodbury	Stagecoach 84/85
8b Horton	Wotton-under-Edge (Stage 7d/8a) Alderley (Stage 8a) Hawkesbury Upton (Stage 8a/8b) Old Sodbury (Stage 8b/9a) Chipping Sodbury	Stagecoach 84/85
8b/9a Old Sodbury	Wotton-under-Edge (Stage 7d/8a) Alderley (Stage 8a) Hawkesbury Upton (Stage 8a/8b) Horton (Stage 8b) Chipping Sodbury Stroud (Selsley Variant; 1.7 miles OR) Bath (Stage 10)	Stagecoach 84/85 Stagecoach 69 Stagecoach 620
9d/10 Cold Ashton	Cheltenham	Pulhams Coaches 832
10 Weston	Bath (Stage 10) Bristol	First Bus 4/4a/4b/19/21/37/39/x39

On the Trail

Costs & budgeting

As vacations go, long-distance trekking in the UK is relatively inexpensive. The walking itself is free as no permits are required. The main components of daily expenditure are food and accommodation/camping: approximate costs are set out below.

	Approximate Cost (subject to change)
Room in pub/inn	£35-70 per person (sharing a double/twin room)
B&B	£35-70 per person (sharing a double/twin room)
Bed in hostel	£20-30 per person
Camping	£5-15 per person
Meal in pub/inn	£12-20
Packed lunch	£6-10
Beer (1 pint)	£5-6

Weather

England has famously green countryside and this beautiful greenery requires plenty of water. The water is, of course, supplied by rain and England's location near the Atlantic Ocean ensures that there is plenty of it: the island bears the brunt of many Atlantic fronts as they make their way eastwards. Accordingly, there is a fair chance that you will experience rain at some point on the CW. Often you can be lucky and walk in perfect conditions but you should always be prepared for wet weather, even in summer.

In summer, the sun in the Cotswolds can be strong with temperatures occasionally reaching 30°C or more. The heat saps your energy but fortunately, the CW has many forested sections where there is plenty of shade. However, there are also long stretches along the high crest of the Cotswold Escarpment where there is little shade. Hot conditions reduce the distance that you can cover each day: dehydration and sunstroke are possibilities and you must carry more water than normal.

The CW runs for 102 miles across England and, at any given time, the weather on one part of the trail can be completely different from the weather on another section: for example, it could be raining in Chipping Campden and sunny in Bath or vice versa.

Always get a weather forecast before setting out. Many internet sites provide forecasts, with a varying degree of reliability. The UK Met Office (www.metoffice.gov.uk) is one of the most reliable as it provides regularly updated localised forecasts for different places along the CW. It also provides, free of charge, an excellent smart-phone app that gives local forecasts.

Maps

In this book, we have included real maps for the entire CW: each stage has 1:25,000 scale maps produced by Ordnance Survey, GB's mapping agency. We believe that these are the finest, and most detailed, maps available. They are perfect for navigating the CW. However, if you would also like sheet maps, there are a number of options:

▶ **OS Explorer 1:25,000:** the maps that are printed in this book are based on OS Explorer sheets. Five sheets are required to cover the entire CW: sheets OL45 (The Cotswolds), 179 (Gloucester, Cheltenham & Stroud), 168 (Stroud, Tetbury & Malmesbury), 167 (Thornbury, Dursley & Yate), and 155 (Bristol & Bath).

▶ **OS Landranger 1:50,000:** five sheets are required to cover the entire CW: 151 (Stratford-upon-Avon), 150 (Worcester & the Malverns), 163 (Cheltenham & Cirencester), 162 (Gloucester & Forest of Dean) and 172 (Bristol & Bath).

▶ **Harvey Cotswold Way XT40:** this 1:40,000 waterproof strip map covers the entire trek.

However, perhaps the best overall solution is to combine the real maps provided in this book with OS's excellent smart-phone app: it provides 1:25,000 maps for the whole of GB and uses GPS to show your location and direction on the map. As the app's maps are the same as those provided in this book, they can be used together seamlessly. In the past, people often uploaded a series of GPS waypoints to their devices. However, because the OS app is so effective (showing both the CW route and your actual location), in our opinion, there is now little point in bothering with GPS waypoint uploads. One month's subscription to the app is only £3.99 so it is ideal for CW walkers.

Paths and waymarking

The CW normally follows clear paths and tracks which are well maintained. In winter, early spring and late autumn, or after sustained periods of rain, some paths can be wet and muddy. However, for much of late spring, summer and early autumn, conditions underfoot are drier. There are also some short sections along minor roads and the CW frequently crosses roads and farm tracks: take care at crossings, looking both ways for traffic.

A typical waymark

Much of the countryside is farmland so there are numerous gates and stiles along the CW. Like many routes in rural England, the CW has plenty of twists and turns as it negotiates rights-of-way through farmland and villages. Consequently, the route has been extremely well marked and navigation is usually straightforward: almost every junction has a sign or an acorn (which is the generic symbol for England's National Trails). You will quickly get into a rhythm, looking for the next waymark every time you pass one. In the route descriptions, we do not highlight every junction because the waymarking is so good: generally, we only mention junctions if they are particularly significant or if there are no waymarks. Bear in mind though that waymarking is at the mercy of the environment: for example, signs and waymarks are occasionally obscured by vegetation or destroyed by falling trees.

The terrain undulates regularly but gradients are rarely very severe. Furthermore, there are few long climbs or descents on the CW except where the route drops down from the escarpment to cross valleys or enter towns/villages and then climbs back up afterwards.

Storing bags

Often walkers from the UK travel to the CW carrying only the gear that they will actually take on the trek. However, trekkers from further afield, and those who want to spend some time elsewhere after the trek, will probably have additional baggage which they need to store while trekking. Normally, a hotel that you have stayed at near the start of the trek will let you store bags until your return: check when booking. At the end of the trek, it is possible to get back to the start by public transport: see 'Returning to the start'. Alternatively, sometimes businesses that offer baggage transfer are also willing to store surplus luggage: see below.

Baggage transfer

Businesses offering baggage transfer services can transport your bags to your accommodation each night so that you only need to carry a small day-pack on the trail. This spares you from the burden of having to carry a heavy backpack and enables you to pack more clean clothes and some luxuries. Most of the companies offering unguided tours can organise baggage transfers. The following businesses offer a baggage transfer service along the entire CW without the requirement to book an unguided tour:

▶ **Carryabag:** www.carryabag.co.uk; info@carryabag.co.uk; 01242 250642

▶ **Cotswold Luggage Transfers:** www.luggage-transfers.co.uk; info@thevolunteerinn.net; 01386 840688

▶ **Sherpa Van:** www.sherpavan.com; info@sherpavan.com; 01748 826917

Fuel for camping stoves/Outdoor shops

Airlines will not permit you to transport fuel so campers who are flying to the UK will need to source it upon arrival, before setting out on the trek. There are outdoor shops in Broadway (Stage 1a/1b), Cheltenham (Stage 3c/3d/4a; 3.5 miles OR), Stroud (Selsley Variant; 1.7 miles OR) and Bath (Stage 10): methylated spirits and standard screw-in gas canisters are normally available but it is wise to call in advance to check.

▶ **Broadway: Landmark Walking** (01386 854995)

▶ **Cheltenham: Blacks** (01242 509855); **Millets** (01242 501008); **Mountain Warehouse** (01242 231586)

► **Stroud: Millets** (01453 700192); **Mountain Warehouse** (01453 766100)

► **Bath: Cotswold Outdoors** (01225 562230); **BCH Outdoor** (01225 460200);
   Blacks (01225 436678); **Millets** (01225 435500);
   Mountain Warehouse (01225 461494); **Bath Outdoors** (01225 251448)

Gas canisters are also usually available in branches of Halfords: there are Halfords stores in Evesham, Cheltenham and Stroud. You can order online for collection in-shop.

If you need petrol or diesel for a multi-fuel stove, there are service stations along the CW at Broadway (Stage 1a/1b), Stonehouse (Stage 6; OR), Stroud (Selsley Variant; 1.7 miles OR), Dursley (Stage 7b/7c), Wotton-under-Edge (Stage 7d/8a), Old Sodbury (Stage 8b/9a), Pennsylvania (Stage 9c/9d) and Bath (Stage 10).

Drinking water

Drinking water will be one of your primary considerations each day. Even in England, the sun can be hot: dehydration and sunstroke are possibilities. Finding water while on the trail can be tricky. You pass relatively few lakes and rivers and anyway, drinking from them is not advisable: farmers in rural England often use pesticides and fertilisers and traces of them may find their way into the watercourses. Water is heavy and therefore it is not always possible to start the day carrying all the water that you will need. Accordingly, you will probably need to take advantage of the many pubs and cafés along the way: many have outdoor taps that you can use and at others, the staff will normally fill your water bottles for free if you ask politely. In fact, licensed premises in England (those that are authorised to serve alcohol) are required by law to provide 'free potable water' to their customers upon request.

Occasionally, there are shops along the way where you can buy water or other drinks. In the introduction to each section, we list these shops and other places where refreshments are available. It is good practice to fill up in the morning at your accommodation, starting the day with at least 1.5 litres. Plan carefully so that you know where your next fill-up point will be. Furthermore, always check your water levels when you pass a source of water.

Ticks

As is often the case in Europe, ticks are present in England. They can carry Lyme disease or tick-borne encephalitis so check yourself regularly. Remove ticks with a tick removal tool (making sure that you get all of it out) and then disinfect the area.

Lambing

Between March and May, many ewes along the CW will be lambing. Trekkers should be particularly careful not to disturb the sheep at this time: do not bring dogs onto land where there are pregnant ewes. If you spot any ewe in distress, or a lamb that appears to have been abandoned, report it to the nearest farmer.

Walking with dogs

Dogs are generally permitted along the route of the CW. However, they should be kept under proper control and during lambing season, you should respect any diversions that farmers put in place. Some hotels/B&Bs accept dogs but others do not: check in advance. Sensible guidelines for dog-owners are as follows.

► Never let your dog worry or attack farm animals

► Do not take a dog into fields where there are lambs, calves or other young farm animals

► If you enter a field containing farm animals, keep your dog on a short lead or close at heel and keep as far as possible from the animals. Take particular care around lambs, calves or other young farm animals

► If cattle react aggressively and move towards you, keep calm, let go of your dog and take the shortest, safest route out of the field

► Do not take a dog into fields of vegetables or fruit unless there is a clear path and keep your dog on the path

► In areas where there are ground-nesting birds, keep your dog on a short lead or close at heel during the breeding season (usually March-July) to avoid disturbing the birds

► In recreation areas and public places, avoid causing concern to others by keeping your dog close at heel or on a short lead

► Pick up and remove your dog's faeces if it defecates in a public open place

Stinchcombe Hill (Stage 7c)

Equipment

The view from Stinchcombe Hill (Stage 7c)

The long-distance trekker has no influence over challenges like weather and terrain but can control the contents of a pack carried on the trail. Some trekkers carry only a light day-pack, paying for a baggage transfer service to transport the bulk of their gear to their nightly accommodation: see 'Baggage transfer'. Many others, however, elect to carry all their own gear and it is fair to say that a lot of those people set off carrying equipment which is unnecessary or simply too heavy: this can result in injury and/or exhaustion, leading to abandonment. If you are intending to carry your own gear, then you should give equipment choice careful consideration: it will be crucial to your enjoyment of the trek and the likelihood of success.

When undertaking any long-distance route, you should be properly equipped for the worst terrain and the worst weather conditions which you could encounter. On the CW, a key consideration is rain: you might not get any in practice but you should expect it when planning. You should carry clothing to combat cold and rain: getting cold and wet in the hills is unpleasant and can be dangerous. Furthermore, even in England, the sun can be strong so you should carry a sun-hat and sun-screen.

However, you should also consider weight and avoid carrying anything unnecessary. The heavier your pack, the harder the trek will be. A trekker's base weight is the weight of his/her pack, excluding food and water. If you are not carrying camping gear and cooking equipment, it is perfectly possible to get by with a base weight of 5-6kg (13lb) or less. If you intend to carry camping equipment then, by investing in some modern lightweight gear, you could start the trek with a base weight of 8-9kg (17lb) or less. Many people are quick to tell you that the lighter the gear, the greater the price but that is not always the case. While it is true that lightweight gear can be expensive, there are also some excellent lightweight products which are great value. Tents, sleeping bags and backpacks are the three heaviest items that you will carry so they offer the biggest opportunities for weight-saving. But do not ignore the smaller items either as the weight can quickly add up. So, if you can afford it, it is sensible to invest some money in gear before you go. The lighter your gear, the more you will enjoy the trek and the better your chance of success. Be ruthless as every ounce counts.

Recommended basic kit

Layering of clothing is the key to warmth: warm air gets trapped between the layers, acting as insulation. Merino wool or man-made materials are preferable: they wick moisture away from the skin, keeping you warm. Do not wear cotton: it does not dry quickly and gets cold.

Boots/Shoes	Good quality, properly fitting and worn in. Robust soles (such as Vibram) are advisable. For the CW, trail-running shoes are adequate but many prefer boots with ankle support. Shoes/boots with a waterproof membrane (such as Gore-Tex) are a good idea.
Socks	2 pairs of good quality, quick-drying walking socks: wash one, wear one. Hand-wash them regularly, helping to avoid blisters. As a luxury, it is nice to have a third pair to wear in the evenings.
Waterproof jacket and trousers	A waterproof and breathable rain jacket is essential although it might never leave your pack. Waterproof over-trousers are also advisable.
Base layers	2 T-shirts and underpants of man-made fabrics or merino wool, which wick moisture away from your body: wash one, wear one. As a luxury, it is nice to have a third set to wear in the evenings.
Fleeces	2 fleeces. Man-made fabrics.
Shorts/ Trousers	2 pairs of shorts or walking trousers. Convertible trousers are practical as you can remove the legs on warm days. One pair of shorts and one pair of trousers is also a good combination in summer.
Warm hat	Always carry a warm hat. Even in summer it can be cold, particularly on windy days.
Gloves	Early or late season trekkers may wish to bring gloves.
Down jacket	Advisable in early spring, autumn and winter when low temperatures are more likely, especially in the evening and early morning.
Camp shoes	It is nice to have shoes to wear in the evenings. Flip-flops or Crocs are a common choice as they are light. However, if you have comfortable hiking boots/shoes then you might consider not bringing camp shoes to save weight.
Waterproof pack liner	Most backpacks are not very waterproof. An internal liner will keep your gear dry if it rains. Many trekkers use external pack covers but we do not find them to be very useful: they flap in the wind and in heavy rain, water still finds its way into the pack around the straps (so you need an internal liner anyway).
Whistle	For emergencies. Many rucksacks have one incorporated into the sternum strap.
Head-light with spare batteries	You will need a flashlight if you are camping. And it is good practice to carry one for emergencies: it can assist if you get caught out late and enable you to signal to rescuers.

Basic first-aid kit	Including plasters, a bandage, antiseptic wipes and painkillers. Blister plasters, moleskin padding or tape (such as Leukotape) can be useful to prevent or combat blisters. A tick removal tool or card is also recommended.
Map and compass	For maps, see page 47. A GPS unit or a smart-phone app can be a useful addition but they are no substitute for a map and compass: after all, batteries can run out and electronics can fail.
Knife	Such as a Swiss Army knife. You are going to need to cut that cheese!
Sunglasses, sun hat, sunscreen and lip salve	Even in England, the sun can be strong so do not set out without these items.
Walking poles	These transfer weight from your legs onto your arms, keeping you fresher. They also save your knees (particularly on descents) and can reduce the likelihood of falling or twisting an ankle.
Phone and charger	A smart-phone is a very useful tool on a trek. It can be used for emergencies. Furthermore, apps for weather, mapping and hotel booking are invaluable. It can also replace your camera to save weight.
Towel	If you are staying at campsites, you will need a towel: lightweight trekking towels are good.
Toiletries	Campers will need to bring soap/shower gel: a small hotel-size bottle should be enough to last the trek, saving a lot of weight. An almost empty toothpaste tube will also save weight. For those who shave, shaving oil is a lightweight alternative to a can of foam/gel. Leave that make-up behind!
Ziplock plastic bag	A lightweight way of keeping money, passport and credit cards dry.
Emergency food	Carry some emergency food over and above your planned daily ration. Energy bars, nuts and dried fruit are all good.
Water	See 'Drinking water' above. Hydration packs with tubes enable drinking on the move.
Toilet paper and trowel	Bring a backpacking trowel in case nature calls on the trail: bury toilet waste and carry out used toilet paper.
Backpack	Your backpack is one of the heaviest items that you will carry. The difference in the weights of various packs can be surprisingly large. 35-40 litres should be sufficient if you are not carrying camping gear. 45-60 litres should be adequate for campers. If you need a pack bigger than these then you are most likely carrying too much. Look for well-padded shoulder straps and waist band. Much of the weight of the pack should sit on your hips rather than your shoulders.

Additional gear for campers

Tent: this is one of the heaviest things that you will carry so it provides a big opportunity for weight saving. Some 2-person tents weigh more than 3kg while others weigh less than 0.6kg. The heaviest ones are normally built for extreme winter conditions and are overkill for the normal CW trekking season. The lightest ones are quite fragile but this is not normally an issue on the CW where campsites are grassy. Although a few premium brands charge a lot for their products and there are some very expensive tents at the lightest end of the scale, these days there are plenty of lightweight tents available at a reasonable price. Tents weighing 1 to 1.5kg often strike a good balance between price, longevity and weight. Consider money spent here as an investment in your well-being and enjoyment of one of the world's great trails. Believe us when we say that a few kgs can be the difference between success and failure.

Your tent should be waterproof to ensure that you stay dry during rainy nights. If you are going to use a very light tent then a footprint can be a good idea to protect its base: 'footprint' is a trendy, modern word for what used to be known as a groundsheet. Sometimes you can buy footprints specific to your tent model but we prefer to use a sheet of Tyvek which can be cut to size: Tyvek is extremely tough and is cheaper, and normally lighter, than most branded footprints.

Tent Pegs: tent weights provided by manufacturers normally exclude the weight of the pegs. The pegs actually provided with tents tend to be quite heavy and many trekkers buy replacement ones which are lighter. Six heavy pegs can weigh as much as 240g while 6 light pegs can weigh as little as 6g. There are many different types available these days and it is important to match the peg with the type of ground they will be used in. The ground on the CW is soft and normally grassy so it is usually easy to get pegs into it. Accordingly, they do not need to be too strong.

Sleeping bag: each bag has a 'comfort rating': This is the lowest temperature at which the standard woman should enjoy a comfortable night's sleep. There is also a 'lower comfort limit' which is for men. That may sound simple but it is not. Although all reputable sleeping bag manufacturers use the same independent standard, the bags are not tested in the same place so there is a lack of consistency amongst ratings. Also, the ratings are designed with an average man and woman in mind but every person is different: some people get colder than others. The ratings should therefore be used as a guide only and it is wise to choose a bag with a comfort rating which is a few degrees lower than the night temperatures that you will encounter. In June, July and August a bag rated at 5-10°C is normally sufficient. In early and late season, you may want something warmer. However, you do not want to bring a bag that is much too warm as that would add unnecessary weight to your pack.

Unfortunately, with sleeping bags, price tends to be inversely proportional to weight. This is largely because the lightest bags are filled with goose/duck down which is expensive. Synthetic bags are also available but they are much heavier so down is a better choice for trekking. The disadvantage of down bags is that they can lose their warmth if they get wet but that is less likely if you have a good tent and pack liner. Our advice is first to decide what comfort rating you will require. Then choose the lightest bag (with that rating) which you can afford.

Sleeping mat: this makes it comfortable for you to sleep on the hard ground and insulates you from the ground's cold surface. There are three types: air, self-inflating and closed-cell foam. The advantages and disadvantages of each are set out below. For the CW, weight is normally more of an issue than warmth so we prefer air mats.

Sleeping Mat Type	Pros	Cons
Air mats: need to be blown up	Lightest Very comfortable Most compact when packed Thicker: good for side sleepers	Most expensive Hard work to inflate Can be punctured Less warm than self-inflating
Self-inflating mats: a combination of air and closed-cell foam. The mat partially inflates itself when the valve is opened	Warmest Very comfortable Quite compact More durable than air mats Firmness is adjustable by adding air	Heavier More expensive than closed-cell foam Can be punctured
Closed-cell foam mats	Light Least expensive Most durable Cannot be punctured	Not compact: needs to be strapped to the outside of your pack Least warm Least comfortable

Pillow: some use rolled-up clothing but we prefer inflatable trekking pillows which only weigh around 50g.

Stove: you should choose a stove that uses a type of fuel which is available on the CW. Airlines do not permit you to carry fuel on planes so, if you are flying to England, you will need to source fuel on arrival. Although methylated spirits are sometimes stocked in outdoor shops, these days gas is more widely available (see 'On the Trail'). Most gas stoves are designed to fit generic screw-on canisters (not Campinggaz) which are readily available in the UK. Canisters for Campinggaz stoves (which are popular in France) are much harder to find so are not a good choice for the CW. Multi-fuel stoves that burn petrol and/or diesel are useful though: the locations of service stations along the CW are listed on page 49.

Hundreds of different stoves are available, some more complicated than others. Often the lightest ones are the most simple and often the most simple ones are relatively inexpensive. If, like most campers, you will eat dried food such as pasta and rice then your stove will need to do little more than boil water. A basic stove which mounts on top of a gas canister will therefore be adequate: such a stove should also be cheap and lightweight (less than 100g).

Pots: if, like most campers, you eat dried food such as pasta and rice then you will only need one pot which will do little more than boil water. To save weight, go for the smallest pot that you can get away with. For example, if you are travelling solo and planning to use freeze-dried backpacking meals then you would need nothing bigger than a 500-600ml pot. Titanium pots are usually the lightest but they are slightly more expensive. Get the lightest one that you can afford.

Fork/Spoon: we love Sporks! They have a spoon at one end and a fork at the other. They weigh only 9g and cost very little.

Safety

*The path around Haresfield Hill
(Stage 6)*

On a calm summer's day, the Cotswolds are paradise. But a sudden weather shift or an injury can change things dramatically so treat the countryside with respect and be conscious of your experience levels and physical capabilities. The following is a non-exhaustive list of recommendations:

► The fitter you are at the start of your trip, the more you will enjoy the hiking.

► Start early to avoid walking during the hottest part of the day and to allow surplus time in case something goes wrong.

► Do not stray from the waymarked paths so as to avoid getting lost and to help prevent erosion of the landscape.

► Before you set out each day, study the route and make plans based upon the abilities of the weakest member of your party.

► Get a weather forecast (daily if possible) and reassess your plans in light of it. Avoid exposed routes if the weather is uncertain.

► Never be too proud to turn back if you find the going too tough or if the weather deteriorates.

► Bring a map and compass and know how to use them.

► Carry surplus food and clothing for emergencies.

► Avoid exposed high ground in a thunderstorm. If you get caught out in one then drop your walking poles and stay away from trees, overhanging rocks, metal structures and caves. Generally accepted advice is to squat on your pack and keep as low as possible.

► In the event of an accident, move an injured person into a safe place and administer any necessary first-aid. Keep the victim warm. Establish your exact coordinates and, if possible, use your cell-phone to call for help. The emergency number is 999. If you have no signal then send someone for help.

► When cooking on a camping stove, place the stove on the ground. Do not use it on a picnic table. We have witnessed a walker knocking over his stove and spilling boiling water on his legs: this is a sure-fire way to end your trek.

General Information

Language: English is the main language.

Charging electronic devices: the UK uses a 3-pin plug. Visitors from outside the UK or Ireland will need an adapter. Some campsites facilitate the charging of electronic devices but this may not be possible at the more basic places. Some people carry their own portable charging devices.

Money: the UK uses Sterling (£). On the CW itself, there are ATMs in Chipping Campden (Stage 1a), Broadway (Stage 1a/1b), Winchcombe (Stage 2c/3a), Painswick (Stage 5/6), Dursley (Stage 7b/7c), Wotton-under-Edge (Stage 7d/8a), Weston (Stage 10) and Bath (Stage 10). Off the main route, there are ATMs at Cheltenham (Stage 3c/3d/4a; 3.5 miles OR), Kings Stanley (Stage 6; 0.3 miles OR) and Stroud (Selsley Variant; 1.7 miles OR). Credit cards are accepted almost everywhere.

Visas: citizens of the European Union, Australia, New Zealand, Canada or the US do not need a visa for short tourist trips to the UK.

Cell-phones: there is generally good network along the CW. Occasionally, however, it can be difficult to get a signal. When network is available, it is likely to be a 3G/4G service enabling access to the internet from smart-phones. In the UK, the roll-out of a new 5G network is underway.

International dialling codes: the country code for the UK is +44. If dialling from overseas, the 0 in UK area codes is omitted.

WiFi: nearly all hotels, pubs and B&Bs have WiFi (see Accommodation Listings). Some campsites do not offer it.

Emergencies and rescue: rescue services are normally free and are provided by unpaid volunteers. The emergency number is 999: ask for 'mountain rescue'.

Insurance: depending upon your nationality, any required medical treatment in the UK may not be provided free of charge so it is wise to purchase travel insurance which covers hiking.

Tourist Information: there are tourist information centres at Chipping Campden (01386 841206; www.chippingcampdenonline.org), Broadway (01386 852937; www.broadway-cotswolds.co.uk), Winchcombe (01242 602925; www.winchcombe.co.uk), Painswick (01452 812278; www.painswicktouristinfo.co.uk) and Wotton-under-Edge (01453 521541). The following websites are useful too:

► **www.visitbath.co.uk:** the official website for the City of Bath

► **www.cotswolds.com:** tourist information for the Cotswolds

► **www.nationaltrail.co.uk:** information on all of England's National Trails, including the CW

► **www.nationaltrust.org.uk:** this charity owns/manages many sites along the CW

► **www.english-heritage.org.uk:** this charity owns/manages many sites along the CW

► **www.cotswoldwayassociation.org.uk:** this charity helps to care for, and improve, the CW

Wildlife

*Arable fields near Ullenwood
(Section 4)*

Much of the fauna in the Cotswolds is similar to that in other parts of the UK. There are roe deer, foxes, badgers, rabbits, grey squirrels, hedgehogs, mice, shrews, voles, stoats, weasels and bats. There are also hares which are often confused with rabbits but in fact, they are quite easy to tell apart: hares have distinctive pointy faces and longer ears (with black tips). There are snakes too: adders (which are venomous) and grass snakes (which are not venomous). Some streams and rivers in the Cotswolds support rare species such as otter and water vole.

However, during spring and summer, the colourful butterflies are more likely to catch your eye. The limestone grassland of the Cotswolds supports a wide variety of wild-flowers upon which butterflies thrive, including rare limestone specialists such as the orange-brown Duke of Burgundy and the Chalkhill Blue (with its pale blue colouring). Furthermore, the beautiful Adonis Blue (with its bright blue wings, fringed with white) has recently been re-introduced. Grassland areas which attract plenty of butterflies include Cleeve Common, Stinchcombe Hill, Prestbury Hill Reserve, Crickley Hill and Painswick Hill.

Plenty of the bird life is also similar to that in other parts of the UK. However, there are also rare species of farmland birds such as skylark, yellowhammer, lapwing and grey partridge. There are woodpeckers and cuckoos too. Easier to spot though are the birds of prey such as buzzards, kestrels, red kites (recognisable by their forked tails) and sparrowhawks: they soar or hover high above, searching for prey.

Plants and Flowers

Fox gloves

The limestone rock in the Cotswolds has helped to create areas of unique limestone grassland which support rare plants and wild-flowers. Unfortunately, only a small fraction of the unimproved limestone grassland survives today, mainly on slopes which are too steep to plough. Cleeve Common, Crickley Hill and Selsley Common are good examples. Flowers include cowslip, violets and orchids.

Hawthorn Blossom

Generally speaking, the types of woodland in the Cotswolds fall into two main groups: firstly, there are the beech woods occurring on the steep slopes of the Cotswold Escarpment; secondly, mixed deciduous woodland occurs on the gentler slopes to the E of the escarpment. Common trees are beech, ash, oak, rowan and hazel. In the hedgerows, hawthorn is seemingly everywhere: those who visit in spring, will be treated to an incredible display of hawthorn blossom. In the woods where soils have been undisturbed for centuries, bluebells occur in vast quantities in April/May. Gorse (which also flowers in spring) is common too: anyone who walks through a section of bright gorse will be struck by the mouth-watering coconut aroma.

Those walking the CW in late summer and early autumn will find plenty of blackberries. Purple sloe berries (which grow on blackthorn) are common too: they look like giant blueberries but they do not taste like them! In fact, sloe berries are only really palatable when added to gin.

History of the Cotswolds

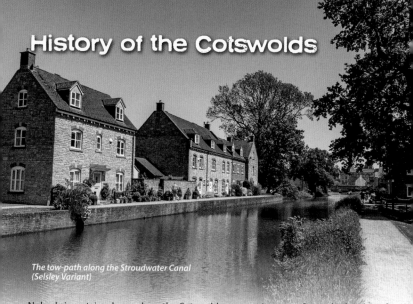

The tow-path along the Stroudwater Canal
(Selsley Variant)

Nobody is certain when or how the Cotswolds area got its name. Some think it dates from Anglo-Saxon times, with 'Cot' being the name of a local Saxon landowner and 'wolds' being the word for 'high lands': so the highlands that Cot owned were 'Cot's wolds'. Others think that 'cots' were a name for sheep enclosures and so 'Cotswolds' meant 'sheep enclosures in the high lands'.

Before the Romans

The Cotswolds have been occupied by humans for at least 5,000 years and some of the walking paths in the region have been in use for a very long time. Originally, much of the Cotswolds was covered with trees and, during the Mesolithic period (c8,000-4,000 BCE), people hunted in the woodland and cleared small sections of trees by burning. During the Neolithic period (c4,000-2,500 BCE), groups of people formed settlements and cleared woodland on a larger scale to facilitate the planting of crops and grazing of livestock. These agricultural settlements grew in number and size during the Bronze Age (c2,500-750 BCE) and the clearing of trees continued. During the Iron Age (750 BCE to 43 CE), communities further expanded and hill-forts were constructed to house and defend larger communities. Many hill-forts have been found in the Cotswolds and the CW passes a number of them.

The Roman period of occupation

During the Roman period (43-407 CE), a lot of food was required to feed the vast Roman army and an ever-increasing population of Roman citizens. To enable systematic exploitation of the land in the Cotswolds for agriculture, they built villas and roads: Great Witcombe Roman Villa is only a stone's throw from the route of Stage 5. The Romans also brought sheep with them to raise for wool: this has great significance in Cotswold history as it was the genesis of the region's wool trade which would later create so much prosperity. During Roman times, there was a thriving economy in the region based on agriculture and trade: wool and corn production were the main activities. Perhaps the most famous legacy of the Romans' period of occupation is the Roman bath complex, which gives the city of Bath its name.

The Saxons

Relatively little is known about life in the Cotswolds in the years following the decline of the Roman Empire. The lack of written materials, coins and pottery means that archaeological evidence is scanty. We do know, however, that when the Romans left, their sheep fell into the hands of the local population who started to trade the wool. We also know that the Saxons invaded England, founding settlements, churches and monastic sites from the end of the 7th century (including those at Bath, Gloucester and Hawkesbury). It is thought that the Saxons further cultivated the land, clearing yet more woodland.

Rise of the wool trade

It is estimated that, by the start of the Norman conquest of England in 1066 CE, two-thirds of the land in the Cotswolds was devoted to arable production. Farming was based on the 'open field' system under which individual tenant farmers cultivated unfenced strips of land. Part of the arable land was left fallow and grazed communally by villagers' sheep and cattle to restore its fertility. The woodlands then remaining were mainly those on slopes too steep to cultivate. Sheep were grazed on the high grasslands of the hills including the Cotswold Escarpment. In Norman times, wool became an important commodity which was sold to continental Europe. In 1348, the 'Black Death' (bubonic plague) wiped out about one-third of the population of the Cotswolds, causing a shortage of the labour required for corn production. Consequently, a lot of arable land was converted to grazing for sheep and the wool industry grew dramatically, generating great wealth for the region.

At the peak of wool production, a significant proportion of the wealth of the entire country came from Cotswold wool. Evidence of the prosperity created by the wool trade can still be seen today: many merchants built fine manor houses with the proceeds and impressive 'wool churches' were constructed in the principal wool-trading towns like Chipping Campden (Stage 1a).

Later, businesses in the region started to add value to the wool by using it to manufacture cloth. Hundreds of new water-mills were built in the valleys to provide power for the industry. From the end of the 18th century, as the industrial revolution gathered pace, mills and factories grew in size to accommodate new machinery. Many new houses, in villages such as Painswick (Stage 5/6), were built for the wool workers around that time.

However, this golden age of Cotswold wool production did not last: around the middle of the 19th century, wool prices collapsed, partly as a result of competition from more efficient steam-powered mills. Many Cotswold mills closed and the workers lost their jobs. For the rest of the 19th century, the Cotswolds suffered an economic decline.

Enclosure

The open field system of agriculture had significant limitations. Because fields were grazed communally when fallow, an individual farmer could not alter his/her methods of farming unless the collective also agreed to do so. As early as the 12th century, some landowners recognised the drawbacks of open fields and enclosed their land into individually owned or rented fields, putting an end to common grazing on it. With larger areas of land, farmers could improve their efficiency and yield. Over the centuries, fewer and fewer tenants farmed larger and larger areas.

In Tudor times (1485 to 1603), enclosure continued as a result of the increasing demand for wool. With large wool profits to be made, manorial lords wanted to increase the acreage available exclusively to them: they enclosed their land (often illegally) and converted it from arable to sheep pasture. Many villagers were evicted and their livelihoods destroyed.

Between 1536 and 1540, Henry VIII shut down and confiscated the Catholic monasteries, priories, convents and friaries in England. In the process, he acquired their land and wealth and destroyed many of the fine buildings. Much of the land was sold off cheaply to nobles who built magnificent houses using the stone from the monastery ruins. They also established huge parks on their land and planted much woodland, reversing the long-standing trend of woodland clearance.

After 1750, enclosure accelerated dramatically as landowners and politicians sought to increase agricultural efficiency. The aim was to turn all land into productive farmland including open fields, common pastures and wasteland. Enclosure was now effected by Acts of Parliament and by 1914, one-fifth of the entire surface area of England had been enclosed in this way. Many more farmers were thrown off their land and forced into employment, either as farm labourers for the landowners or (as the industrial revolution gathered pace) factory workers. By the end of the 19th century, most of the common land in England had been enclosed.

These Parliamentary enclosures had a significant and lasting impact on the visual landscape and character of the Cotswolds: on the ground, landowners implemented enclosure by the construction of dry-stone walls, or the planting of hedgerows, around the fields. It is these dry-stone walls, and the beautiful patchwork of fields that they created, that CW trekkers marvel at today. Many landowners also built new stone cottages in the local villages for their workers to live in: many of these still survive too.

The 20th century

The economic and agricultural depression in the Cotswolds during the second half of the 19th century was halted by the Great War (1914-1918). Cloth mills were re-purposed to manufacture essential goods such as agricultural equipment. After the war, Cotswold agriculture benefited greatly from the availability of new machines such as steam engines and mechanical reapers. Access to the region improved too with the construction of many new tarmac roads. During WW2, efforts to dramatically increase food production saw large swathes of pastures and old limestone grassland ploughed up and turned into arable land. That fundamentally changed the landscape of the Cotswolds in a way that would never be reversed.

After WW2, food shortages meant that the government continued to encourage intensive arable farming and more limestone grassland and pasture was ploughed-up. At that time, knowledge of archaeological sites was limited and sadly, many hill-forts and burial grounds were destroyed in the process. Prior to WW2, approximately 40% of the Cotswolds was permanent pasture but today, the level is less than 2%. With less land available for grazing, and the preference of modern farmers for dairy and beef farming, comparatively few sheep now remain.

Sadly, the post-war years have also seen a decline in the network of dry-stone walls. Sometimes, walls were removed to create bigger fields (which are more suitable for efficient arable production using modern machinery). In other cases, walls fell into disrepair through lack of maintenance. Those that survive help to foster the unique character that makes the Cotswolds so popular with visitors today. Tourism in the Cotswolds is booming and it is estimated that about 16 million people visit the region each year, contributing more than £1 billion to the local economy.

Chipping Campden/ Stanton

1

The old wool-trading town of Chipping Campden is an excellent place to start/finish the CW. For many, it is the Cotswolds in a nutshell: historic buildings of honey-coloured stone which are a mere stone's throw from lovely green fields and rolling hills. The town centre is packed with history and modern life has not managed to dim its charm and character. The town was built (on the profits of wool) between the 14th and 17th centuries using locally quarried stone. For further information on Chipping Campden and its sights, see page 70 or www.chippingcampdenonline.org.

The CW officially starts/finishes at the elegant Market Hall which was built in 1627 as a market for traders selling goods such as dairy products and cloths. It is owned by the National Trust. In front of the SW end of it, set into the stone flags, there is a CW marker stone carved with the names of places along the trek. Inscribed around the outer ring of the stone is a quotation from T.S. Eliot's Four Quartets: "Now the light falls across the open field, leaving the deep lane shuttered with branches, dark in the afternoon". Next to the stone, there is an old milestone for Bath.

Section 1 is a visual treat, involving three of the finest settlements in the Cotswolds as well as classic Cotswold countryside and plenty of lovely dry-stone walls. There is so much to take in that it is barely possible to do it

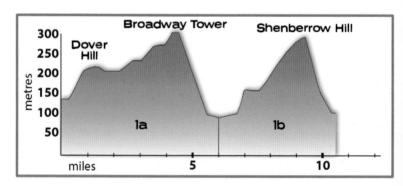

The village green in
Broadway (Stage 1a/1b)

justice in a day. From Chipping Campden, N-S hikers climb to the superb
viewpoint on Dover's Hill. From there, a lovely journey through farmland
leads you to the much-photographed Broadway Tower which, after Cleeve
Hill, is the second highest point on the CW: the views are breathtaking on
a clear day. A steep descent through flower-filled pastures and grassland
brings you to the town of Broadway (see page 73) which is completely
unlike Chipping Campden but just as beautiful: its broad tree-lined main
street is flanked by shops, pubs, cafés and wisteria-attired cottages, all
built from honey-coloured limestone. It found fame as a stagecoach stop
on the route from London to Worcester. It is a lovely place for a break or an
overnight stay, although it can get quite busy with day-trippers. However,
do not linger too long because, between Broadway and Stanton, there is
more exquisite countryside to enjoy. S-N trekkers, of course, view Stanton
first, then Broadway and finish the trek at Chipping Campden.

Stanton is a real treat and some claim that it is the most beautiful village in
the whole region: accommodation is limited (so book well in advance) and
there is only one place to eat. However, Chipping Campden and Broadway
both have plenty of places to stay/eat and both have supermarkets where
you can stock up on supplies.

The route is well marked and navigation is straightforward. There is quite a
lot of climbing and descending so many N-S hikers (who are not yet 'trail-
hardened') prefer to split Section 1 into two stages, with an overnight stop
in Broadway: this also makes good sense if you are starting from Chipping
Campden in the afternoon and do not want to rush on to Stanton that day.

		Time	Distance	Ascent N-S	Descent N-S
Stage 1a	Chipping Campden/ Broadway	2:45	6.0miles 9.6km	538ft 164m	702ft 214m
Stage 1b	Broadway/ Stanton	2:00	4.5miles 7.3km	692ft 211m	627ft 191m

Supplies/Water:

Chipping Campden (Stage 1a) - supermarket, shops, pharmacy & ATMs
Broadway (Stage 1a/1b) - supermarkets, shops & ATMs

Refreshments/Food:

Chipping Campden (Stage 1a) - restaurants, pubs, tea rooms & coffee shops
Broadway Tower (Stage 1a) - Morris & Brown Café
Broadway (Stage 1a/1b) - restaurants, pubs, tea rooms & cafés
Stanton (Stage 1b/2a) - the Mount Inn

The Market Hall in Chipping Campden (Stage 1a)

Accommodation:
Chipping Campden (Stage 1a) - hotels, pubs & B&Bs
Broadway (Stage 1a/1b) - hotels, pubs & B&Bs
Stanton (Stage 1b/2a) - B&Bs

Escape/Access:
Chipping Campden (Stage 1a) - bus
Broadway (Stage 1a/1b) - bus; GWSR heritage railway
Stanton (Stage 1b/2a) - bus

⑤ Broadway Tower

This limestone folly with its turrets, battlements and gargoyles was designed by architect James Wyatt for the 6th Earl of Coventry. It was completed in 1798. Set high on the Cotswold Escarpment, it is one of the region's most iconic landmarks. In 1822, it was bought by Sir Thomas Phipps who set up a printing press within it. Later pre-Raphaelite artists such as William Morris, Dante Gabriel Rossetti and Edward Burne-Jones used it as a holiday retreat.

During the 20th century, it was used by the Royal Observer Corp as an observation tower for tracking aircraft. Today, the tower is still in private hands but is open to the public (entrance fee): it is worth climbing to the rooftop balcony from which you can apparently see 16 of England's counties. A memorial stone nearby marks the spot where a Whitley bomber crashed in 1943, killing its crew. There is also a Cold War nuclear bunker near the tower, built to study the effects of nuclear explosions and the resulting radioactive fallout: it was also manned by the Royal Observer Corp until it closed in 1991. You can visit the bunker on a guided tour. For further information on the tower and bunker, see **www.broadwaytower.co.uk**.

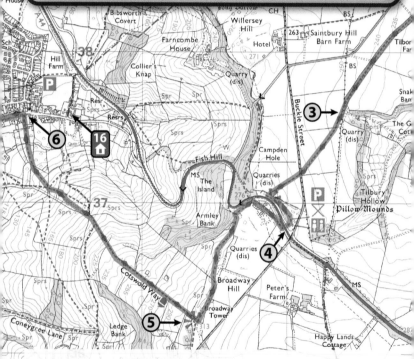

N-S

Stage 1a: Chipping Campden to Broadway

S From the CW marker stone at the **Market Hall**, walk SW along **High Street**. TR after **St Catherine's Church** onto **Back Ends/Hoo Lane**. Soon start to climb out of the village on a track.

1 0:25: TL along a road. Shortly afterwards, cross over and TR on a path. 5min later, go through a kissing gate and TL. Shortly afterwards, pass the trig point on **Dover's Hill**: there is a bench nearby with lovely views.

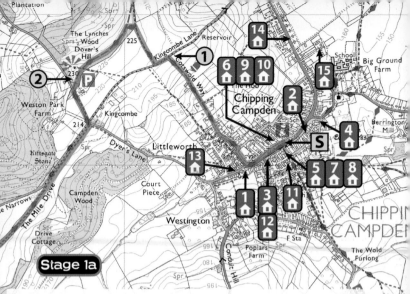

② 0:35: Go through a gate and keep SH through a car park. Just before a road, TL on a path. A few minutes later, keep SH across a road junction. Immediately afterwards, TR on a path alongside a road. 10min later, climb a stone stile and TL on a path.

③ 1:20: Keep SH into a field. 5-10min later, cross a road and keep SH into another field. At the end of the field, TL on a path. Just afterwards, TR at a fork. Keep SH through a flat grassy area with picnic benches. Shortly afterwards, keep SH past **Fish Hill** parking area.

④ 1:40: Just afterwards, TR. Shortly afterwards, TL on a lane.

⑤ 2:05: TR at **Broadway Tower** (see box) and descend on a path.

⑥ 2:40: TL along **High Street**.

Ⓕ 2:45: Arrive in the centre of **Broadway**.

S-N

Stage 1a: Broadway to Chipping Campden

Ⓕ Head E along **High Street**.

⑥ 0:05: TR on a lane which soon becomes a path. Climb grassy slopes.

⑤ 0:50: TL at **Broadway Tower** (see box) and descend on a path.

④ 1:10: Cross a road. Just afterwards, keep SH past **Fish Hill** parking area. Keep SH through a flat grassy area with picnic benches. TR onto a path through a field. Cross a road and continue through another field.

③ 1:30: 5-10min later, leave the field, continuing on a path. Later, TL, cross a road junction and pick up a path heading NW (parallel to a road).

② 2:10: Shortly, keep SH through a car park and go through a gate. Then bear right and head NE along **Dover's Hill**. A few minutes later, pass a trig point: there is a bench nearby with lovely views. Soon afterwards, TR and go through a kissing gate.

① 2:25: TL along a road. Shortly afterwards, TR on a path. TL and walk NE along **High Street** in **Chipping Campden**.

Ⓢ 2:45: Arrive at the **Market Hall**. Congratulations! You have completed the CW.

What to see in Chipping Campden

▶ **Market Hall** (see page 64).

▶ **Grevel House** was the home of William Grevel, one of England's most influential wool merchants. It is located at the N end of the High Street and was built in 1380.

▶ **Woolstaplers Hall**, opposite Grevel House, was built in 1340 and was used as a wool exchange.

▶ **St. James's Church** is one of the finest of the 'wool churches' in the Cotswolds and is around 500 years old. Each of the lime trees in the church ground represents one of the 12 apostles.

▶ **Campden House Gateway** is beside St. James's Church. You can still see the lodge and gateway of the old Campden House (which burnt down during the Civil War).

▶ **The almshouses on Church Street** were built in 1612 by Sir Baptist Hicks whose coat of arms is visible on the face of the row. An 'almshouse' was a unit of residential accommodation belonging to a charity or wealthy benefactor. These particular almshouses were designed to house poor men and women and are still used by pensioners today.

The lovely village of Stanton (Stage 1b/2a)

N-S

Stage 1b: Broadway to Stanton

S Head W along **High Street**. From the **village green**, head S on **Church Street**. Pass the **Crown and Trumpet pub**. Shortly afterwards, TR onto a path. 5-10min later, cross a road and continue uphill on a path.

1 0:30: TL onto a farm track. 10min later, TR in a farmyard and continue on a path: the waymarking is not clear. 5min later, ignore a path on the left and keep SH through a gate. Just afterwards, ignore a path on the right.

2 1:20: TL onto a lane. Immediately afterwards, TR on a track.

3 1:35: Go through a gate beside a farmhouse. Just afterwards, keep SH (ignoring a path on the right). Soon start to descend.

4 1:50: TL on a track.

F 2:00: Arrive in **Stanton**.

S-N

Stage 1b: Stanton to Broadway

F Head E along **High Street**.

4 0:15: TR at a junction and climb.

3 0:30: Keep SH (ignoring a path on the left). Just afterwards, go through a gate beside a farmhouse.

2 0:45: TL on a lane. Immediately afterwards, TR at a junction. 30min later, ignore a path on the left. Just afterwards, keep SH through a gate and ignore a path on the right. 5min later, TL in a farmyard and continue on a track: the waymarking is not clear.

1 1:30: 10min later, pick up a path on the right, leaving the track. 15min later, cross a road. TL along **Church Street**. Pass the **Crown and Trumpet Pub**.

S 2:00: Arrive at the **village green** in **Broadway**.

Stanton

With its honey-coloured limestone houses and delightfully traffic-free streets, Stanton is perhaps the textbook Cotswold village. The fact that there are no shops or services (other than the **Mount Inn**) enhances the peaceful atmosphere as does the regular sight of horses trotting along the streets. Some of the buildings were built in the 16th century and there is a **medieval cross** in the middle of the village. **St Michael's Church** probably dates back to the 9th century but the current structure is mostly 15th century.

Stage 2a

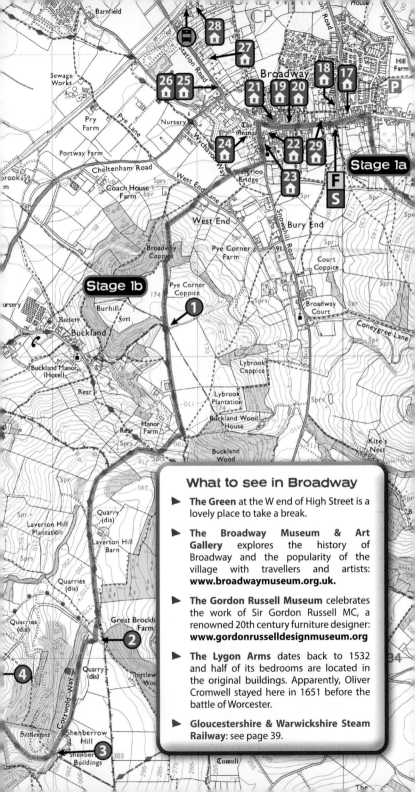

Stage 1a

Stage 1b

F
S

What to see in Broadway

▶ **The Green** at the W end of High Street is a lovely place to take a break.

▶ **The Broadway Museum & Art Gallery** explores the history of Broadway and the popularity of the village with travellers and artists: **www.broadwaymuseum.org.uk.**

▶ **The Gordon Russell Museum** celebrates the work of Sir Gordon Russell MC, a renowned 20th century furniture designer: **www.gordonrusselldesignmuseum.org**

▶ **The Lygon Arms** dates back to 1532 and half of its bedrooms are located in the original buildings. Apparently, Oliver Cromwell stayed here in 1651 before the battle of Worcester.

▶ **Gloucestershire & Warwickshire Steam Railway**: see page 39.

Section 2 is an excellent showcase for the wonderful scenery of the CW. Classic Cotswold countryside is on display, viewed from fabulous vantage points high on the Cotswold Escarpment: rolling hills and a patchwork of fields bordered by beautiful dry-stone walls of honey-coloured limestone. There is hawthorn seemingly everywhere and in spring, its pale blossom is a sight to behold. There are plenty of historic sights too. The CW passes through the stunning village of Stanway with its lovely church: take the time to visit Stanway House, a Jacobean manor with beautiful gardens (see page 79). And you will visit Cromwell's Seat, a monument on the spot where Thomas Cromwell once stood as he watched Hailes Abbey burn (see page 80). The remains of the abbey are also along the trail and are well worth a visit.

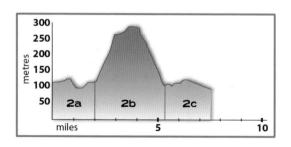

The medieval cross in Stanton (Stage 1b/2a)

Winchcombe is full of character and has plenty of places to stay and eat. The Winchcombe Folk and Police Museum is interesting (www.winchcombemuseum.org.uk) but the historic Sudeley Castle (see page 81) is unmissable if you have a few hours to spare. The Gloucestershire & Warwickshire Steam Railway stops in Winchcombe: see page 39.

For S-N trekkers, Stanton is a lovely place to spend the night, however, accommodation is limited so book well in advance: there is only one place to eat.

The route is generally well marked and navigation is straightforward. For N-S trekkers, the climb out of Wood Stanway is quite taxing. On Stage 2c, between ① and ②, the waymarking is poor and the route is sometimes tricky to follow.

		Time	Distance	Ascent N-S	Descent N-S
Stage 2a	Stanton/ Wood Stanway	0:45	2.0miles 3.2km	69ft 21m	66ft 20m
Stage 2b	Wood Stanway/ Hayles Fruit Farm	1:45	3.3miles 5.3km	515ft 157m	505ft 154m
Stage 2c	Hayles Fruit Farm/ Winchcombe	1:00	2.2miles 3.6km	105ft 32m	184ft 56m

The lovely village of Stanway (Stage 2a)

Supplies/Water:

Hayles Fruit Farm (Stage 2b/2c) - farm shop (groceries, sandwiches & drinks)

Winchcombe (Stage 2c/3a) - supermarkets, bakery, shops & ATMs

Refreshments/Food:

Stanton (Stage 1b/2a) - the Mount Inn

Stanway (Stage 2a) - tea room at Stanway House

Hayles Fruit Farm (Stage 2b/2c) - tea room (breakfast; lunch; evening meals a few times a week - pizza or fish & chips)

Winchcombe (Stage 2c/3a) - pubs, restaurants & cafés

Accommodation:

Stanton (Stage 1b/2a) - B&Bs

Wood Stanway (Stage 2a/2b) - Wood Stanway Farmhouse B&B

North Farmcote B&B (Stage 2b; 0.2 miles OR)

Hayles Fruit Farm (Stage 2b/2c) - camping

Ireley Farm B&B (Stage 2c; 0.6 miles OR)

Winchcombe (Stage 2c/3a) - pubs & B&Bs

Escape/Access:

Stanton (Stage 1b/2a) - bus

Toddington (Stage 2a; 0.9 miles OR from Stanway) - GWSR heritage railway

Hailes Abbey halt (Stage 2c; 0.5 miles OR) - GWSR heritage railway

Winchcombe (Stage 2c/3a) - bus; GWSR heritage railway

N-S

Stage 2a: Stanton to Wood Stanway

S Head S along **Stanway Road**. A few minutes later, TL on a lane, climbing gently. Shortly afterwards, TR, go through a gate and keep SH through a long narrow field, following waymarks on posts. 5min later, go through a gate and continue on a path.

1 0:30: TL along a minor road. Shortly, reach the hamlet of **Stanway** (see box). Shortly after the church and the S gatehouse of **Stanway House**, TL on a lane. Shortly afterwards, keep SH on a path, passing an old mill. A few minutes later, TL on a footpath alongside a road. Shortly afterwards, TR (crossing the road) and continue on a path.

F 0:45: Arrive at a junction in the hamlet of **Wood Stanway**. TL to start **Stage 2b** or TR for **Wood Stanway Farmhouse B&B**.

S-N

Stage 2a: Wood Stanway to Stanton

F From the junction in **Wood Stanway**, head N on a path. Cross a road and TL along a path beside it. Shortly afterwards, TR on a path. Shortly after passing an old mill, TR on a road and enter the village of **Stanway** (see box). Pass the gatehouse of **Stanway House** and a church.

1 0:15: TR onto a path. Follow waymarks on posts through fields. When you reach the village of **Stanton**, TL on a lane. Shortly afterwards, TR along **Stanway Road**.

S 0:45: Arrive in the centre of **Stanton**.

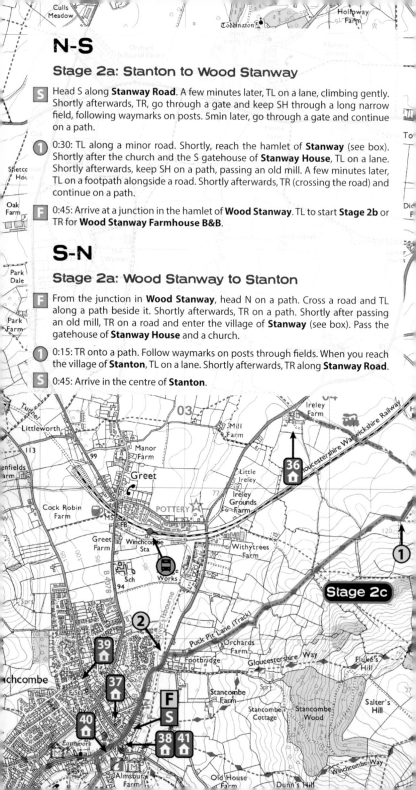

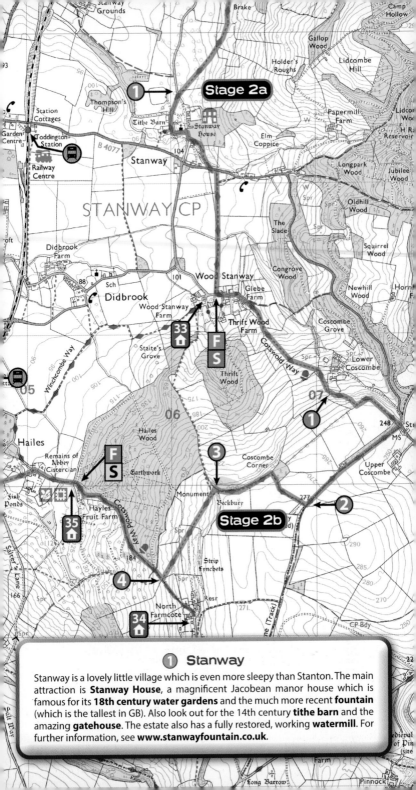

Stage 2a

Stage 2b

① Stanway

Stanway is a lovely little village which is even more sleepy than Stanton. The main attraction is **Stanway House**, a magnificent Jacobean manor house which is famous for its **18th century water gardens** and the much more recent **fountain** (which is the tallest in GB). Also look out for the 14th century **tithe barn** and the amazing **gatehouse**. The estate also has a fully restored, working **watermill**. For further information, see **www.stanwayfountain.co.uk**.

N-S

Stage 2b: Wood Stanway to Hayles Fruit Farm

S From the junction in **Wood Stanway**, head E on a lane. A few minutes later, TR onto a track. A few minutes later, go through a gate and climb on a path.

1 0:25: TL, go through a gate and continue uphill on a narrow path. 10min later, TR at a road. Immediately afterwards, TR onto a track.

2 0:55: TR at a junction. Soon, TR along the side of a field. TL at the far corner of the field. Soon pass **Beckbury Camp**, the site of an Iron Age hill-fort

3 1:15: TR at a **monument** (known as **Cromwell's Seat**: see box) and descend on a steep and narrow path.

4 1:30: Go through a gate and TR on a track: alternatively, TL for **North Farmcote B&B**.

F 1:45: Arrive at the entrance to **Hayles Fruit Farm**.

Stage 2c: Hayles Fruit Farm to Winchcombe

S From the entrance to **Hayles Fruit Farm**, descend NW on a lane. A few minutes later, pass **Hailes Abbey** (see box). Just afterwards, TL on a path through a field. At the end of the field, keep SH on a lane. Then TR along a minor road. A few minutes later, TL on a track.

1 0:20: TR on a muddy path. 10min later, go through a gate and keep SH through a field (no path): cross the brow of a hill, descend and cross a bridge over muddy terrain. It is easy to get lost on this section. After the bridge, bear right downhill through another field, towards a gate. Keep SH on a track.

2 0:50: Cross a road and then TL on a footpath alongside it.

F 1:00: Arrive in **Winchcombe**.

3 Cromwell's Seat

At the NW corner of the **Beckbury Camp hill-fort**, there is a spring. On the site of the spring, there is a **limestone monument**, built in the 19th century, with alcoves and basins. On the side of the monument there is a protruding stone slab known as '**Cromwell's Seat**' because it is believed that in 1539, on this spot, Thomas Cromwell watched Hailes Abbey burning in the valley below (following its dissolution).

Hailes Abbey

Hailes Abbey was consecrated in 1251 and occupied by the Cistercian Order of monks. In 1270, the monks were presented with the **Holy Blood of Hailes**: this holy relic was a crystal container believed to hold a portion of the blood of Christ. The E side of the church was re-built shortly afterwards to house the relic. Afterwards, the abbey became a place of pilgrimage. The relic became famous throughout the country and **Chaucer** mentioned it in '**The Canterbury Tales**'. In 1538, the Bishop of Worcester had the relic sealed in a box and taken to London for examination. Later that year, it was declared that it was nothing more than clarified honey coloured with saffron. Soon afterwards, the shrine in the abbey was stripped of its valuables and dismantled. In 1539, the monks surrendered the abbey to Henry VIII and it was soon reduced to ruins. The abbey is well worth a visit (entrance fee except for English Heritage or National Trust members). For further information, see **www.english-heritage.org.uk**.

S-N

Stage 2c: Winchcombe to Hayles Fruit Farm

F From **Winchcombe**, head N on **Hailes Street**.

(2) 0:10: TR onto **Puck Pit Lane**. After a while, go through a gate and then climb across the middle of a field: look out for a bridge in the left boundary of the field (easy to miss). Cross the bridge over muddy terrain. Then head NE across the brow of a hill. Go through a gate at the other side of the field.

(1) 0:40: 10min later, TL onto a track. 5-10min later, TR on a road. Shortly afterwards, TL on a lane. Then keep SH across a field. At **Hailes Abbey** (see box), TR and climb SE on a lane.

S 1:00: Arrive at the entrance to **Hayles Fruit Farm**.

Stage 2b: Hayles Fruit Farm to Wood Stanway

F From the lane at the entrance to **Hayles Fruit Farm**, head SE, climbing on a track.

(4) 0:20: TL and climb on a path: alternatively, keep SH for **North Farmcote B&B**.

(3) 0:40: Head E from a **monument** (known as **Cromwell's Seat**: see box) and walk along the left side of a field. This is the site of **Beckbury Camp Iron Age hill-fort**. TR at the far corner of the field.

(2) 1:00: TL at a junction. After a while, TL at a road. Immediately afterwards, TL onto a path.

(1) 1:25: Go through a gate and then bear right.

S 1:45: Arrive at a lane in **Wood Stanway**. Head W until you reach a junction: TR on a path to start **Stage 2a** or keep SH for **Wood Stanway Farmhouse B&B**.

Sudeley Castle

Sudeley Castle was once a royal residence, closely associated with many English monarchs including Edward IV, Richard III, Henry VIII, Elizabeth I and Charles I. Queen Katherine Parr, the last wife of Henry VIII, lies entombed within the castle's church. Charles I sheltered in the castle during the Civil War: after the war, it lay derelict for 200 years. In 1837, John and William Dent, Worcester glove-makers, started to restore the buildings. It is now the home of Lady Ashcombe and her family. Today, you can explore the beautiful gardens, St Mary's Church and many parts of the castle itself including the 15th century west wing. For tickets and information, see www.sudeleycastle.co.uk.

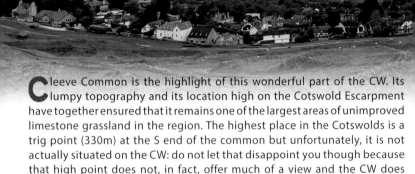

3 Winchcombe/Ham Hill

Cleeve Common is the highlight of this wonderful part of the CW. Its lumpy topography and its location high on the Cotswold Escarpment have together ensured that it remains one of the largest areas of unimproved limestone grassland in the region. The highest place in the Cotswolds is a trig point (330m) at the S end of the common but unfortunately, it is not actually situated on the CW: do not let that disappoint you though because that high point does not, in fact, offer much of a view and the CW does visit Cleeve Common's other trig point (317m) which is only slightly lower and which does provide fabulous views over Cheltenham, the Malverns and the Severn Valley. You will also pass the still-visible outline of an Iron Age hill-fort just above Nutterswood and a Bronze Age territorial boundary known as the Cross Dyke.

Cleeve Common is a Site of Special Scientific Interest. It is privately owned and managed by a charitable trust. Today, the biggest threat to its areas of old grassland is under-grazing: without the sheep and cattle that still roam the common, coarse grasses, hawthorn and gorse would overwhelm the wide variety of wild-flowers which are magnificent in spring and summer. The common also supports a wide variety of mammals, reptiles, butterflies and birds. For further information, see www.cleevecommon.org.uk.

Elsewhere, away from Cleeve Common, there is more classic Cotswold scenery to enjoy: rolling hills, dry-stone walls and flower-infused hedgerows. And then there is Belas Knap, one of the most impressive long barrow burial mounds in the whole of the UK, which dates back to around 3,000 BCE.

Cleeve Hill has some good places to stay, however, you will have to descend

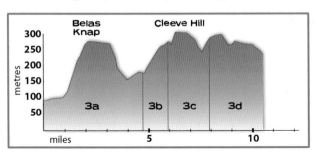

The view from Cleeve Common (Stage 3c)

off the Cotswold Escarpment to get to them: you can eat at the Rising Sun pub or Cleeve Hill Golf Club. Section 3 finishes at Colgate Farm near Ham Hill: to get to Colgate Farm B&B/campsite, you will need to follow a signed path that runs a short distance W of the CW. Alternatively, Whittington Lodge Farm B&B is about 1.5 miles E of ④. You could also descend into Charlton Kings (1.5 miles OR) where there are places to stay and eat.

Another option is to stay in Cheltenham where there is a much wider variety of accommodation and restaurants. There are many paths off the CW that head towards the town: we have indicated on the route map one possible option from Stage 3c which entails a 3.5 mile walk (much of which is alongside roads). However, it would perhaps be preferable to descend off the escarpment to a road (perhaps in Charlton Kings) and arrange for a taxi to pick you up from there and take you into the centre of Cheltenham. For detailed information on places to stay in Cheltenham, see www.visitcheltenham.com.

For S-N walkers, Winchcombe is a lovely place to end the day. It is full of character and has plenty of good pubs where you can overnight and eat. For more information on Winchcombe, see page 75.

The route is well marked and navigation is straightforward. However, take care to follow the waymarks on Cleeve Common which has a complicated labyrinth of paths. N-S trekkers should be aware that, after Winchcombe, there are no shops on the CW until Painswick (Stage 5/6).

		Time	Distance	Ascent N-S	Descent N-S
Stage 3a	Winchcombe/ Postlip	2:30(N-S) 2:15(S-N)	4.7miles 7.6km	751ft 229m	466ft 142m
Stage 3b	Postlip/ Cleeve Hill	0:45(N-S) 0:30(S-N)	1.2miles 2.0km	302ft 92m	26ft 8m
Stage 3c	Cleeve Hill/ Upper Hill Farm exit	1:00	2.0miles 3.2km	302ft 92m	289ft 88m
Stage 3d	Upper Hill Farm exit/ Ham Hill	1:15	2.5miles 4.1km	197ft 60m	325ft 99m

Supplies/Water:

Winchcombe (Stage 2c/3a) - supermarkets, bakery, shops & ATMs

Charlton Kings (Stage 3d/4a; 1.5-1.9 miles OR) - supermarkets & pharmacy

Cheltenham (Stage 3c/3d/4a; 3.5 miles OR) - supermarkets, pharmacies, shops & ATMs

Refreshments/Food:

Winchcombe (Stage 2c/3a) - pubs, restaurants & cafés

Postlip (Stage 3a/3b) - Postlip Pitstop at Postlip Hall Farm (ice cream & drinks; irregular hours)

Cleeve Hill (Stage 3b/3c) - Cotswold Way Café beside the Cleeve Hill Golf Club; restaurant at Cleeve Hill Golf Club; Rising Sun pub (0.3 miles OR)

Charlton Kings (Stage 3d/4a; 1.5-1.9 miles OR) - pubs

Cheltenham (Stage 3c/3d/4a; 3.5 miles OR) - pubs, restaurants & cafés

Postlip Hall (Stage 3b)

Accommodation:

Winchcombe (Stage 2c/3a) - pubs & B&Bs

Postlip (Stage 3a/3b) - B&Bs

Cleeve Hill (Stage 3b/3c) - pub, hotel & B&B (all 0.3 miles OR)

Upper Hill Farm B&B (Stage 3c/3d; 0.5 miles OR)

Ham Hill (Stage 3d/4a) - B&B & camping

Charlton Kings (Stage 3d/4a; 1.5-1.9 miles OR) - pub & B&B

Cheltenham (Stage 3c/3d/4a; 3.5 miles OR) - hotels & B&Bs

Escape/Access:

Winchcombe (Stage 2c/3a) - bus; GWSR heritage railway

Cleeve Hill (Stage 3b/3c) - bus

Charlton Kings (Stage 3d/4a; 1.5-1.9 miles OR) - bus

Cheltenham (Stage 3c/3d/4a; 3.5 miles OR) - bus; train

③ *Belas Knap Long Barrow (Stage 3a)*

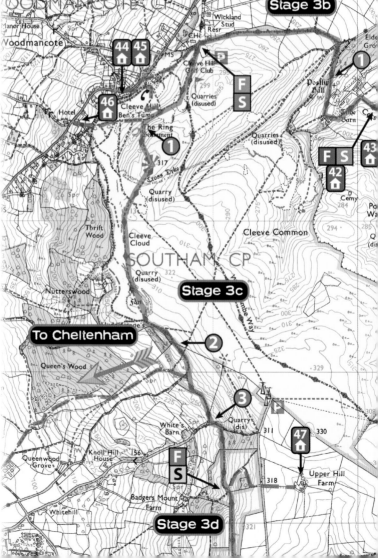

Stage 3b

Stage 3c

To Cheltenham

Stage 3d

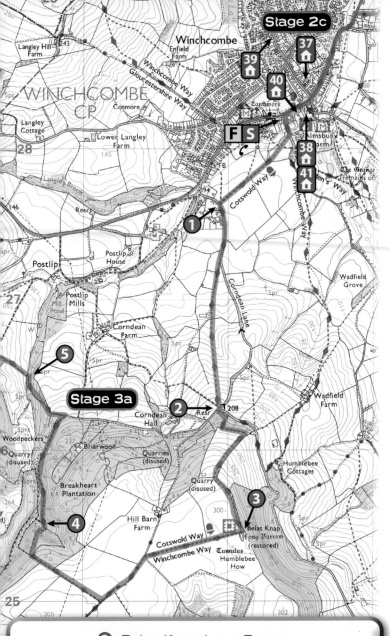

Winchcombe

Enfield Farm

Langley Hill Farm

Winchcombe Way

WINCHCOMBE CP

Gloucestershire Way

Cotmore

Langley Cottage

Lower Langley Farm

Langley Brook

Resr

Postlip

Postlip House

Postlip Mills

Mill Pond

Corndean Farm

Woodpeckers

Quarry (disused)

Briarwood

Quarries (disused)

Breakheart Plantation

Hill Barn Farm

Quarry (disused)

Corndean Hall

Corndean Lane

Cotswold Way

Winchcombe Way

Wadfield Grove

Wadfield Farm

Humblebee Cottages

Belas Knap Long Barrow (restored)

Tumulus Humblebee How

West Down

Wood

3 Belas Knap Long Barrow

Belas Knap is a **Neolithic long barrow burial mound** which was probably built around 3000 BCE. It has been substantially restored. It was first excavated in 1863. The main entrance on the N side is a dummy: the burial chambers are actually accessed from the sides and would have been invisible from the outside when covered with earth. Four burial chambers have been identified and the remains of 31 people have been found.

N-S

Stage 3a: Winchcombe to Postlip

S From the centre of **Winchcombe**, head SW along the B4632. TL down **Vineyard Street**. A few minutes later, TR on a path.

1 0:20: TL along a minor road. At the entrance to **Corndean Hall**, go through a gate and TL on a lane. 5-10min later, TL on a path and climb through a field.

2 0:50: Cross a road and continue uphill on a path through trees. At the top of the slope, go through a gate and TL on a path along the side of a field. At the far side of the field, TR and climb alongside a dry-stone wall.

3 1:20: At **Belas Knap Long Barrow** (see p87), go through the right-hand gate: the waymarks are confusing. Then TR and head SW on a path alongside a dry-stone wall. 10min later, TL on a path. 5min afterwards, TR onto a path along the side of a field. At the end of the field, go through a gate and descend on a path.

4 1:50: Keep SH at a junction. 10min later, keep SH on a lane. Shortly afterwards, TL on a path and descend again.

5 2:15: TL across a footbridge and go through a gate. Then climb on a path along the side of a field. Soon, go through a gate, TR and climb on a track. A few minutes later, TL into a field to go around a farmyard: soon return to the track.

F 2:30: Arrive at **Postlip Hall Farm B&B**.

Stage 3b: Postlip to Cleeve Hill

S From **Postlip Hall Farm B&B**, descend NW on a lane: notice **Postlip Hall** up ahead. Shortly afterwards, TL on a path. Keep SH through a farmyard. At a junction, TR. Then go through a gate.

1 0:15: Go through a gate and climb. A few minutes later, keep SH at a diagonal junction and head uphill on a broad path. After a few minutes, the path bends left. Shortly afterwards, go through a gate and continue on a track. A few minutes later, keep SH at a junction.

F 0:45: Just after **Cleeve Hill car park**, reach a junction of paths beside **Cleeve Hill Golf Club**. Descend SW on a path to head to the Cleeve Hill accommodation or head S on a path to start **Stage 3c**.

Stage 3c: Cleeve Hill to Upper Hill Farm exit

S From the junction at **Cleeve Hill Golf Club**, head S on a path and climb across **Cleeve Common**: there are two paths heading S and you should take the right-hand one.

1 0:15: At a junction, take the second of two paths heading uphill to the left: climb steeply. 5min later, TR at a **trig point (317m)**: this is the highest point on the CW. Now follow a broad grassy path through the golf course, following waymarks on posts: watch out for golf balls. You should see **Cheltenham Racecourse** below. Pass an Iron Age hill-fort.

2 0:45: Go through a gate on the right. Immediately afterwards, TL at a fork on a narrow path. After a few minutes, the path bends right and descends. Shortly afterwards, TL at a fork: it is easy to go wrong here. Now as you descend, take care to follow waymarks, ignoring paths to the left and right.

3 0:55: TL and climb on a path. Shortly afterwards, TR at a fork. Soon enter **Prestbury Hill Reserve**.

F 1:00: Reach a junction: keep SH and head S to start **Stage 3d** or TL for **Upper Hill Farm B&B**.

S-N

Stage 3c: Upper Hill Farm exit to Cleeve Hill

F From the junction, head N on a path.

3 0:05: TR at a junction. As you climb, take care to follow waymarks, ignoring paths to the left and right. After a while, the path bends right, heading N: it soon bends left again.

2 0:20: Go through a gate and continue NW. Pass an Iron Age hill-fort. You should see **Cheltenham Racecourse** below. Now follow a broad grassy path through the golf course, following waymarks on posts: watch out for golf balls. TL at a **trig point (317m)**: this is the highest point on the CW. Soon, descend steeply.

1 0:45: A few minutes later, TR at a junction and follow a path heading generally N.

S 1:00: Reach a junction of paths beside **Cleeve Hill Golf Club**. Descend SW on a path to head to the Cleeve Hill accommodation or descend E on a track to start **Stage 3b**.

Stage 3b: Cleeve Hill to Postlip

F From **Cleeve Hill Golf Club**, descend E on a track. After 15min, bear right and descend S on a path. At a diagonal junction, choose the path descending S.

1 0:20: Go through a gate. Shortly after going through another gate, TL at a junction. Head through a farmyard. TR and climb on a lane.

S 0:30: Shortly afterwards, arrive at **Postlip Hall Farm B&B**.

Stage 3a: Postlip to Winchcombe

F From **Postlip Hall Farm B&B**, head SE on a lane. Soon, TR into a field to go around a farmyard and then return to the lane. A few minutes later, TL, go through a gate and descend along the side of a field.

5 0:15: Cross a footbridge. Then TR and climb on a path. TR on a lane.

4 0:45: Keep SH on a path which soon climbs. Enter a field and follow a path along the side of it. At the end of the field, TL at a junction, heading NE. 5min later, TR on a path alongside a dry-stone wall.

3 1:20: At the NE corner of **Belas Knap Long Barrow** (see p87), TL and go through a gate. Then head N on a path. Descend along the side of a field: TL at the bottom of it. A few minutes later, TR, go through a gate and descend.

2 1:40: Cross a road and descend through a field. Keep SH on a lane. At the entrance to **Corndean Hall**, go through a gate and TL on a minor road.

1 2:00: TR on a path. TL up **Vineyard Street**.

S 2:15: TR and head NE along the **B4632** into **Winchcombe**.

A carpet of wild-flowers in spring (Stage 3d)

N-S

Stage 3d: Upper Hill Farm exit to Ham Hill

S From the junction, head S on a path. Later, TR at a fork.

(1) 0:20: TL at a junction. Shortly afterwards, TR.

(2) 0:25: Go through a gate and keep SH on a lane. Just afterwards, TL on a path. 5min later, TL along a minor road. TR at the next junction. 10min later, pass a path on the right that heads to the **Coachhouse** at Glenfall House.

(3) 0:50: Soon afterwards, TR onto a path.

(4) 1:10: Keep SH across **Ham Road** and continue S on a path to the left of a farm lane. Alternatively, TL and head E along the road for **Whittington Lodge Farm B&B**.

F 1:15: Reach a junction: keep SH to start **Stage 4a** or TR for **Colgate Farm/Charlton Kings**.

S-N

Stage 3d: Ham Hill to Upper Hill Farm exit

F From the junction, head N on a path.

(4) 0:05: Keep SH across **Ham Road** and continue N on a path. Alternatively, TR and head E along the road for **Whittington Lodge Farm B&B**.

(3) 0:25: TL along a lane. Soon afterwards, pass a path on the left that heads to the **Coachhouse** at Glenfall House. 10min later, TL at a junction. 5min later, TR on a path.

(2) 0:50: TR on a lane. Just afterwards, go through a gate and head NE.

(1) 0:55: TL onto a lane. Shortly afterwards, TR and head N on a path.

S 1:15: Reach a junction: keep SH and head N to start **Stage 3c** or TR for **Upper Hill Farm B&B**.

Lineover Wood seen from Colgate Farm (Stage 3d/4a)

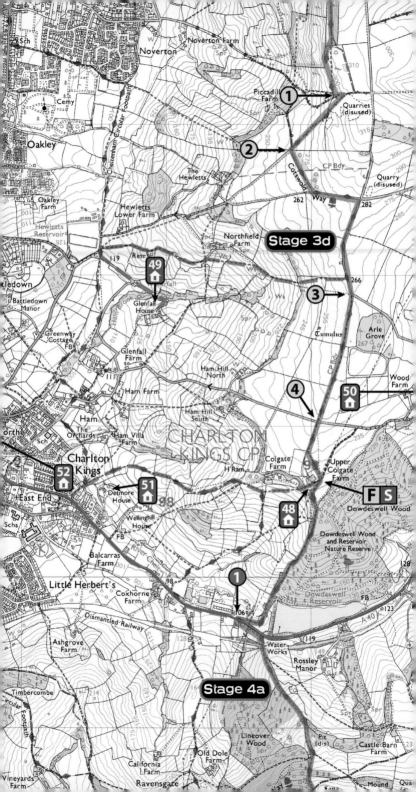

Stage 3d

Stage 4a

4 Ham Hill/Birdlip exit

Most of this section is spent high on the Cotswold Escarpment and the views are some of the best on the CW. A clear highlight is Crickley Hill which is owned by the National Trust: as well as the sublime panorama at the top, you can still see the ridges of the Iron Age hill-fort that once stood on this lofty perch. The grassy summit is covered with wild-flowers in spring and is a lovely place for a picnic. And the CW follows the line of a beautiful section of dry-stone walling along the S side of the hill. Leckhampton Hill and Charlton Kings Common also have fabulous views: Cheltenham lies below and you can see for miles as you walk along the edge of the slopes.

For N-S trekkers, accommodation is limited so book well in advance. There are camping pods at Ullenwood or you can stay at the Royal George Hotel in Birdlip.

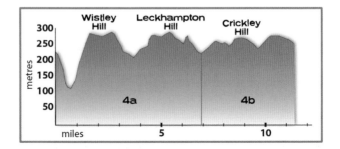

Escarpment views on Stage 4b

S-N trekkers can stay at Colgate Farm B&B/campsite near Ham Hill: follow a signed path that runs a short distance W of the CW. Or consider Whittington Lodge Farm B&B: it is about 1.5 miles E of **4** (which is a short distance further N along the CW on Stage 3d). You could also stay/eat in Charlton Kings: 0.8 miles NW of **1** along the busy A40.

Alternatively, Cheltenham has a much wider variety of places to stay and eat: from **1**, you could walk NW along the A40 (3.5 miles) but it would be preferable to arrange a taxi from there into Cheltenham. For detailed information on places to stay in Cheltenham, see www.visitcheltenham.com.

The route is largely well marked and navigation is normally straightforward. However, at Seven Springs, the waymarking is poor so follow the directions carefully. This section is quite tiring because the route undulates relentlessly as it follows the line of the escarpment.

		Time	Distance	Ascent N-S	Descent N-S
Stage 4a	Ham Hill/Ullenwood	3:45	6.9miles 11.1km	1034ft 315m	1050ft 320m
Stage 4b	Ullenwood/ Birdlip exit	2:15	4.4miles 7.1km	410ft 125m	325ft 99m

Supplies/Water:

Charlton Kings (Stage 3d/4a; 0.8 miles OR) - supermarkets & pharmacy

Cheltenham (Stage 3d/4a; 3.5 miles OR) - supermarkets, pharmacies, shops & ATMs

Refreshments/Food:

Charlton Kings (Stage 3d/4a; 0.8 miles OR) - pubs

Cheltenham (Stage 3d/4a; 3.5 miles OR) - pubs, restaurants & cafés

Dowdeswell Reservoir (Stage 4a) - Koloshi Indian Restaurant

Seven Springs (Stage 4a) - the Cotswold Diner; the Seven Springs

Ullenwood (Stage 4a/4b) - Star Bistro

Crickley Hill Country Park (Stage 4b) - café

The Air Balloon pub (Stage 4b)

Birdlip (Stage 4b/5; 0.1 miles OR) - Royal George Hotel

Accommodation:

Ham Hill (Stage 3d/4a) - B&B & camping

Charlton Kings (Stage 3d/4a; 0.8 miles OR) - pub & B&B

Cheltenham (Stage 3d/4a; 3.5 miles OR) - hotels & B&Bs

Ullenwood (Stage 4a/4b) - Star Glamping

Birdlip (Stage 4b/5; 0.1 miles OR) - Royal George Hotel

Escape/Access:

Charlton Kings (Stage 3d/4a; 0.8 miles OR) - bus

Cheltenham (Stage 3d/4a; 3.5 miles OR) - bus; train

Seven Springs (Stage 4a) - bus

Birdlip (Stage 4b/5; 0.1 miles OR) - bus

Wistley Hill (Stage 4a)

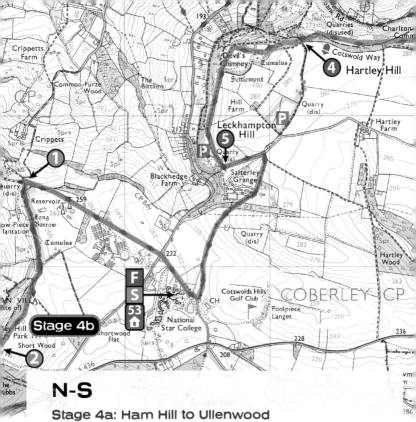

N-S

Stage 4a: Ham Hill to Ullenwood

S From the junction, descend on a path through trees. 15min later, TL across a bridge. Immediately afterwards, TR on a track. A few minutes later, TL on a path.

1 0:25: Shortly afterwards, cross a road at **Koloshi Indian Restaurant** and pick up a path. Soon pass through a parking area and climb on a path into **Lineover Wood** (ancient woodland). After exiting the woods, walk along the N side of **Wistley Plantation**: the views are magnificent.

2 1:25: Reach a signpost where there are five options: bear left and head W on a path into woods. Do not turn sharp left directly into the woods. 5min later, TL and enter a field. Immediately afterwards, TR and walk along the edge of it. At the end of the field, TL and walk SE along its SW side. At the far side of the field, keep SH, descending on a path through trees: the bluebells in spring are wonderful. At a road, turn sharp right to pick up a path running along the side of a field.

3 1:55: Arrive at **Seven Springs** where there are two restaurants. Keep SH across the busy **A435** and then TR along a minor road behind it (no waymarks). 10min later, keep SH on a path. A few minutes later, TL at a junction. Just afterwards, TL at a fork and climb onto **Charlton Kings Common**.

4 2:45: TR and go through a gate. Immediately afterwards, keep SH at a junction, heading along the edge of woods. A few minutes later, TL at a fork. Soon, pass the trig point on **Leckhampton Hill**: then walk towards a topograph where the views are better. From there, continue S along the edge of the hill.

5 3:10: After descending briefly, TL up a minor road. 5min later, TR on a track.

F 3:40: TR onto a road. A few minutes later, arrive at the entrance for **Star Glamping/Star Bistro**.

Victorian post box

S-N

Stage 4a: Ullenwood to Ham Hill

F From the entrance for **Star Glamping/Star Bistro**, head SE on a road. A few minutes later, TL on a track. TL down a minor road.

5 0:25: A few minutes later, TR and climb on a path along the W side of **Leckhampton Hill**. TR at a topograph (which has magnificent views). Shortly afterwards, pass a trig point: afterwards follow a path NE along the edge of woods.

4 1:00: Go through a gate. Shortly afterwards, bear right and head E along **Charlton Kings Common**. After a while, the path bends right again and descends SE. TR onto a broad path. A few minutes later, keep SH on a road.

3 1:40: Arrive at Seven Springs where there are two restaurants. Keep SH across the busy **A435** and pick up a path heading NE along the side of a field. When you leave the field at a road (**A436**), climb NE on a path through trees: the bluebells in spring are wonderful. Enter a field and walk NW along the side of it. At the far side of the field, TR and walk along its NW side. Before the end of the field, TL and leave it: then TR and head N alongside the field boundary. At the end of the field, TR and head E on a path through trees.

2 2:20: TR at a 5-way junction and head E: the views are magnificent. Head E into **Lineover Wood** (ancient woodland). After a while, TL and descend N.

1 3:10: Soon after a parking area, reach a road at **Koloshi Indian Restaurant**: you can TL and walk along the road to get to **Charlton Kings** but there is a lot of traffic. However, to continue on the CW, cross the road and pick up a path. Shortly afterwards, TR onto a track. A few minutes later, TL and cross a bridge. Then climb on a path through trees.

S 3:45: Reach a junction: keep SH to start **Stage 3d** or TL for the path to **Colgate Farm/Charlton Kings**.

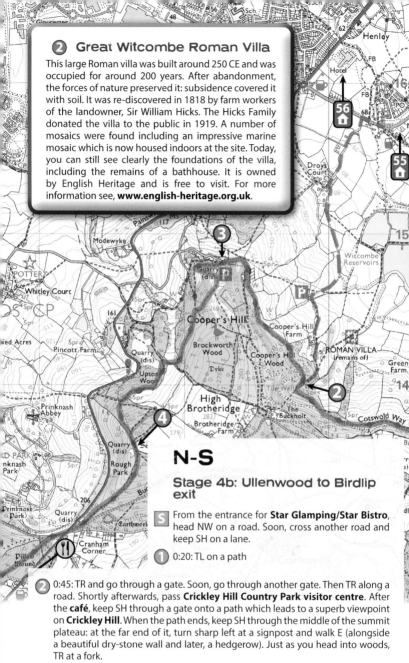

② Great Witcombe Roman Villa

This large Roman villa was built around 250 CE and was occupied for around 200 years. After abandonment, the forces of nature preserved it: subsidence covered it with soil. It was re-discovered in 1818 by farm workers of the landowner, Sir William Hicks. The Hicks Family donated the villa to the public in 1919. A number of mosaics were found including an impressive marine mosaic which is now housed indoors at the site. Today, you can still see clearly the foundations of the villa, including the remains of a bathhouse. It is owned by English Heritage and is free to visit. For more information see, **www.english-heritage.org.uk**.

N-S

Stage 4b: Ullenwood to Birdlip exit

S From the entrance for **Star Glamping/Star Bistro**, head NW on a road. Soon, cross another road and keep SH on a lane.

① 0:20: TL on a path

② 0:45: TR and go through a gate. Soon, go through another gate. Then TR along a road. Shortly afterwards, pass **Crickley Hill Country Park visitor centre**. After the **café**, keep SH through a gate onto a path which leads to a superb viewpoint on **Crickley Hill**. When the path ends, keep SH through the middle of the summit plateau: at the far end of it, turn sharp left at a signpost and walk E (alongside a beautiful dry-stone wall and later, a hedgerow). Just as you head into woods, TR at a fork.

③ 1:20: Cross a busy road at a roundabout. Then TR along the S side of the **Air Balloon pub**: walk up a footpath beside the **A417**. 5min later, TR onto a path.

④ 1:55: Go through a gate and enter forest. Immediately afterwards, TR on a path.

F 2:15: Arrive at a road: cross over and descend on a path to start **Stage 5**. Alternatively, for **Birdlip**, TL and head up the road: take care as there is no footpath.

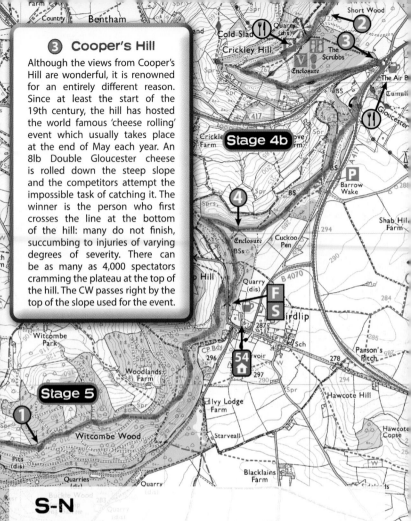

③ Cooper's Hill

Although the views from Cooper's Hill are wonderful, it is renowned for an entirely different reason. Since at least the start of the 19th century, the hill has hosted the world famous 'cheese rolling' event which usually takes place at the end of May each year. An 8lb Double Gloucester cheese is rolled down the steep slope and the competitors attempt the impossible task of catching it. The winner is the person who first crosses the line at the bottom of the hill: many do not finish, succumbing to injuries of varying degrees of severity. There can be as many as 4,000 spectators cramming the plateau at the top of the hill. The CW passes right by the top of the slope used for the event.

S-N

Stage 4b: Birdlip exit to Ullenwood

F Cross over the road and pick up a path heading N through woods.

④ 0:20: Keep SH (E) at a junction and go through a gate. At the **A417**, TL and descend alongside it on a footpath.

③ 0:55: At a roundabout beside the **Air Balloon pub**, TL and cross a busy road. Then pick up a path heading W through woods. When you emerge from the trees, follow a path W alongside a hedgerow and later, a beautiful dry-stone wall. From a signpost at the W end of **Crickley Hill**, turn sharp right and walk E over the summit. Pick up a path heading NE and soon, reach **Crickley Hill Country Park visitor centre** and **café**. Head NE along a road. Shortly afterwards, TL on a path.

② 1:30: Go through a gate and TL.

① 1:55: TR onto a lane. At a road junction, head SE on a road.

S 2:15: Arrive at the entrance for **Star Glamping/Star Bistro**.

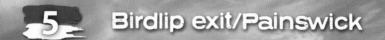

5 Birdlip exit/Painswick

This section of the CW may be short but there is a lot to see. You will spend plenty of time on the crest of the Cotswold Escarpment, sometimes exploring lovely deciduous woodland and, at other times, enjoying expansive panoramas from open grassland. Perhaps the best view of the day is from the wonderful Painswick Beacon (just OR) where you can still see the tell-tale contours of an Iron Age hill-fort. But Cooper's Hill is beautiful too although, rather than savouring the panorama, you will find yourself marvelling at the steep slope that plays host to the annual 'cheese rolling' event (see page 99). On Section 5, the daily serving of history takes the form of the remains of Great Witcombe Roman Villa which is only a short distance OR (see page 98).

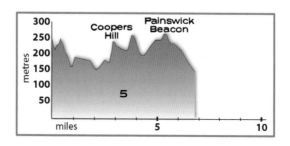

The amazing view from
Painswick Beacon (Stage 5)

However, the highlight of Section 5 is perhaps the village of Painswick which is one of the finest and best-preserved settlements on the entire trek. There are plenty of historical buildings (many of which owe their existence to the wool trade) and the limestone is a noticeably paler colour than that seen in the villages further N. The interesting sights and the excellent pub help to make Painswick our favourite town on the CW: for further information, see page 105. It has some lovely B&Bs too and a campsite just E of the town. However, for trekkers heading N from Painswick, the only accommodation on Section 5 is the Royal George Hotel at Birdlip.

The entire section is well marked and navigation is straightforward. S-N trekkers should note that after Painswick, there are no shops on the CW until Winchcombe (Stage 2c/3a). The timings below include the short side-trip to Painswick Beacon.

		Time	Distance	Ascent N-S	Descent N-S
Stage 5	Birdlip exit/ Painswick	3:30 (N-S) 3:45 (S-N)	6.8miles 10.9km	925ft 282m	1240ft 378m

Supplies/Water:

Painswick (Stage 5/6) - supermarket, pharmacy & ATM

Refreshments/Food:

Birdlip (Stage 4b/5; 0.1 miles OR) - Royal George Hotel

Little Witcombe (Stage 5; 1.5 miles OR) - Twelve Bells Beefeater; Toby Carvery Brockworth

The Royal William pub (Stage 5; 0.1 miles OR from ⑤)

The Waypoint Bar & Kitchen (Stage 5; ⑧)

Painswick (Stage 5/6) - the Oak pub; St Michaels Bistro; the Falcon; Painswick Pooch Coffee House; café at Painswick Rococo Garden

Accommodation:
Birdlip (Stage 4b/5; 0.1 miles OR) - Royal George Hotel
Little Witcombe (Stage 5; 1.5 miles OR) - hotels
Painswick (Stage 5/6) - B&Bs & camping

Escape/Access:
Birdlip (Stage 4b/5; 0.1 miles OR) - bus
Painswick (Stage 5/6) - bus

The wonderful town of Painswick
(Stage 5/6)

N-S

Stage 5: Birdlip exit to Painswick

S Cross the road and descend on a path. Soon, TL at a junction. Take care following waymarks through **Witcombe Wood**: there is a complicated labyrinth of paths.

1 0:35: TR at a junction. Soon notice **Great Witcombe Roman Villa** below to the right.

2 1:05: TL at a fork and climb briefly: alternatively, TR and descend to head to **Great Witcombe Roman Villa** (see page 98)/**Little Witcombe**. Later, keep SH on a lane.

3 1:20: TL and immediately afterwards, bear right onto a path. Soon, TL at a junction and climb steeply. TR on **Cooper's Hill** (see page 99) and head SW on a path: ignore the path heading SE. Descend steeply to a junction: TL.

4 2:00: Just after the sign for **Buckholt Wood**, TR at a junction. 10min later, TR along a minor road. At **Cranham Corner**, cross the A46 and pick up a path heading SW through woods: follow waymarks carefully. Soon, cross a lane and keep SH. Immediately afterwards, TL at a fork.

5 2:25: Keep SH on a lane: alternatively, TL for the **Royal William pub**. 5min later, TR at a fork. Shortly afterwards, TL onto a path. Soon, keep SH on a broad grassy path through a golf course: watch out for golf balls.

6 2:50: Keep SH on the main path to head directly to **7**. Alternatively, TR on one of the paths that climb through the Iron Age hill-fort to **Painswick Beacon**: from the beacon, proceed to **7** by descending S on one of the paths along the ridges of the hill-fort.

7 3:05: At a junction, TL down a lane. Shortly afterwards, TR at a junction. Soon the path runs to the left of a fence beside a quarry.

8 3:15: Pass the **Waypoint Bar & Kitchen** at Painswick Golf Club. 5-10min later, TR on a lane. Shortly afterwards, TR through a parking area and descend on a path. Soon, TR down a road. Shortly afterwards, TL on a footpath alongside **Gloucester Road**. At a junction, TR (remaining on Gloucester Road).

F 3:30: Arrive in the centre of **Painswick**.

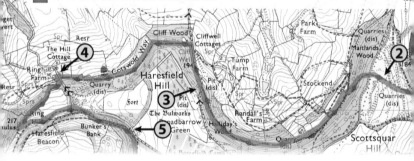

The Iron Age hill-fort at Painswick Beacon (Stage 5)

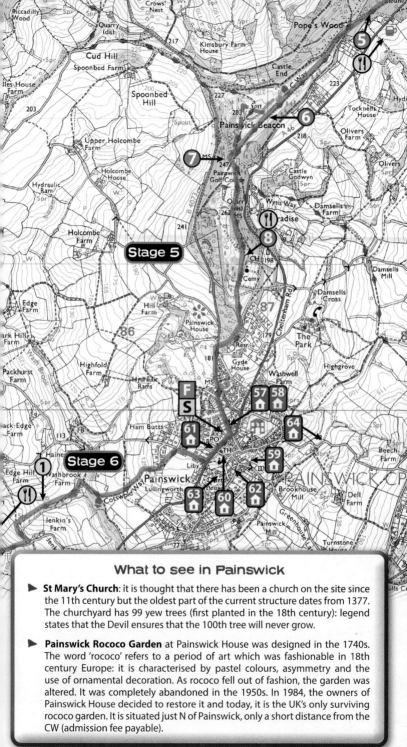

What to see in Painswick

▶ **St Mary's Church**: it is thought that there has been a church on the site since the 11th century but the oldest part of the current structure dates from 1377. The churchyard has 99 yew trees (first planted in the 18th century): legend states that the Devil ensures that the 100th tree will never grow.

▶ **Painswick Rococo Garden** at Painswick House was designed in the 1740s. The word 'rococo' refers to a period of art which was fashionable in 18th century Europe: it is characterised by pastel colours, asymmetry and the use of ornamental decoration. As rococo fell out of fashion, the garden was altered. It was completely abandoned in the 1950s. In 1984, the owners of Painswick House decided to restore it and today, it is the UK's only surviving rococo garden. It is situated just N of Painswick, only a short distance from the CW (admission fee payable).

Stage 5: Painswick to Birdlip exit

F From the centre of **Painswick**, climb N on **Gloucester Road**. TR onto **Golf Course Road**. Shortly afterwards, TL through a parking area and then return to **Golf Course Road**. Shortly after that, TL on a path heading N.

8 0:30: Head N past the **Waypoint Bar & Kitchen** at Painswick Golf Club. When you emerge from the trees near a quarry, TR. Shortly afterwards, keep SH up a lane.

7 0:45: Just afterwards, TR at a junction. Shortly afterwards, keep SH to head directly to **6**. Alternatively, TL to climb through the Iron Age hill-fort to **Painswick Beacon**: from the beacon, proceed to **6** by descending E on one of the paths through the hill-fort.

6 1:00: Head NE on a broad grassy path through **Painswick Golf Course**: watch out for golf balls. After the golf course, keep SH on a lane (heading NE).

Cooper's Hill of 'cheese-rolling' fame (Stage 5)

5 1:20: TL on a path, heading NE: alternatively, stay on the lane for the **Royal William pub**. Follow the waymarks carefully through the woods. At **Cranham Corner**, cross the A46 and head NE on a minor road. Shortly afterwards, TL on a path.

4 1:45: Keep SH at a junction. After a while, TR at a junction and climb steeply to arrive on **Cooper's Hill** (see page 99). Now descend steeply on a path.

3 2:25: From a junction, head E on a lane. Soon, keep SH on a path.

2 2:40: Keep SH at a junction: alternatively, TL and descend to head to **Great Witcombe Roman Villa** (see page 98)/**Little Witcombe**.

1 3:00: TL at a junction. Take care following waymarks through **Witcombe Wood**: there is a complicated labyrinth of paths.

S 3:45: TR at a junction and climb to a road: cross over and pick up a path to start **Stage 4b**. Alternatively, for **Birdlip**, TR and head up the road: take care as there is no footpath.

Painswick/Middleyard

On a clear day, the escarpment hike around Haresfield Hill and the descent towards Stonehouse are highlights of the CW. The far-reaching views from the balcony path near Haresfield Beacon are exceptional and, as you spend a lot of time above the tree-line, you can enjoy them at your leisure. Haresfield Beacon is also home to one of the CW's many Iron Age hill-forts. In spring, the carpets of wild-flowers on the grassy slopes and plateaus are magnificent: there are plenty of good spots for a picnic.

N-S trekkers have two options when they reach the Stroudwater Canal near Stonehouse **10**. The main route of the CW continues S to Middleyard, passing King's Stanley on the way: both villages have places to stay. However, if you have the time and energy, the Selsley Variant is the route

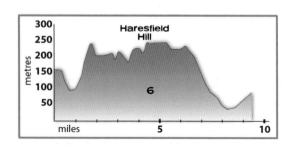

Haresfield Beacon (Stage 6)

to choose for two reasons: firstly, the walk over Selsley Common is sublime and, for many, a highlight of the CW. And secondly, the tow-path along the canal is lovely and completely different to the scenery elsewhere on the trek. The variant re-joins the main CW in Pen Wood ❶, just above Middleyard: from there, you can either continue S on Stage 7a or descend briefly to Middleyard to spend the night. For S-N trekkers, the Selsley Variant is described on page 121.

Middleyard and Kings Stanley have a few B&Bs or you could stay at the pub in nearby Leonard Stanley. Along the Selsley Variant, the Bell Inn (in the village of Selsley) is a lovely place to stay/eat. For S-N trekkers, Painswick is one of the finest and best-preserved settlements on the entire trek (see page 101): it has some lovely B&Bs and a campsite just E of the town.

The section is well marked and navigation is straightforward except between ❽ and ❿ where you will need to follow the directions carefully to avoid losing your way.

		Time	Distance	Ascent N-S	Descent N-S
Stage 6	Painswick/ Middleyard	5:15 (N-S) 5:30 (S-N)	9.4miles 15.2km	1125ft 343m	1352ft 412m

Supplies/Water:

Painswick (Stage 5/6) - supermarket, pharmacy & ATM

Kings Stanley (Stage 6; 0.4 miles OR) - supermarket & ATM; Dangerfields Bakery

Dudbridge (Selsley Variant; 0.2 miles OR) - supermarket

Stroud (Selsley Variant; 1.7 miles OR) - supermarket, outdoor shops, pharmacy & ATM

Refreshments/Food:

Painswick (Stage 5/6) - the Oak pub; St Michaels Bistro; the Falcon; Painswick Pooch Coffee House; café at Painswick Rococo Garden

The Edgemoor Inn (Stage 6)

Randwick (Stage 6; 0.3 miles OR) - the Vine Tree Inn

Westrip (Stage 6; 0.2 miles OR) - the Carpenters Arms

Stonehouse (Stage 6; 0.6 miles OR) - restaurants

Kings Stanley (Stage 6; 0.4 miles OR) - King's Head pub; Ben's Takeaway

Leonard Stanley (Stage 6; 0.9 miles OR) - the White Hart pub

Ebley Wharf (Selsley Variant) - Kitsch Coffee and Wine Bar

Stroud (Selsley Variant; 1.7 miles OR) - restaurants, pubs & cafés

Selsley (Selsley Variant) - the Bell Inn

The contours of the Iron Age hill-fort on Haresfield Hill (Stage 6)

Accommodation:

Painswick (Stage 5/6) - B&Bs & camping

Kings Stanley (Stage 6; 0.4 miles OR) - B&Bs

Leonard Stanley (Stage 6; 0.9 miles OR) - the White Hart pub

Middleyard (Stage 6/7a) - Valley Views B&B

Stroud (Selsley Variant; 1.7 miles OR) - Premier Inn Stroud hotel

Selsley (Selsley Variant) - the Bell Inn

Escape/Access:

Painswick (Stage 5/6) - bus

Stonehouse (Stage 6; 0.6 miles OR) - bus; train

Kings Stanley (Stage 6; 0.4 miles OR) - bus

Middleyard (Stage 6/7a) - bus

Ebley (Selsley Variant) - bus

Stroud (Selsley Variant; 1.7 miles OR) - bus; train

Selsley (Selsley Variant) - bus

N-S

Stage 6: Painswick to Middleyard

S Head SW along **New Street**. TR on **Edge Road**. A few minutes later, TL on a path. Just after passing **Washbrook Farm** (an old mill), TL at a junction. A few minutes later, TL on a path.

(1) 0:30: Go through a gate and TL. Shortly afterwards, keep SH past a CW **stone marker**, heading towards a gate: go through the gate and TL. A few minutes later, TR up a lane. TR alongside the **A4173**. Shortly afterwards, at the **Edgemoor Inn**, cross the road and continue uphill on a path.

(2) 1:05: Approaching the top of the hill, TL. Shortly afterwards, go down steps. Soon, cross a road and descend on a path through **Maitlands Wood**. A few minutes later, TL on a track.

(3) 1:45: Emerge from the woods and descend on a path beside a lane. 5min later, TL and climb on a path. Soon, pass the **Cromwell Stone** which commemorates the raising of the siege of Gloucester in 1643.

(4) 2:10: TL up a steep road. Shortly afterwards, TR and climb on a path. Turn sharp left at **Haresfield Beacon** and walk along the edge of a beautiful ridge.

(5) 2:30: TL at a fork. Shortly afterwards, TR just before a car park and descend some steps: at the bottom, TL on a path. 5min later, TR at a junction. Soon, when the path splits, keep to the middle one, aiming for a topograph. Turn sharp left at the **topograph**.

(6) 3:00: Enter a car park. Shortly afterwards, TR on a path. Shortly after that, TL at a three-way fork. 10min later, TR at a junction.

(7) 3:30: TR at a junction. Soon, TL at a fork. Shortly afterwards, TR.

(8) 3:50: Keep SH across a track onto a path. 5-10min later, TL at a fork (easy to miss). 5min later, TL down a lane. Immediately afterwards, TR and head across a field: take the more easterly of two paths. Soon, TR on a road. A few minutes later, TL and descend on a path.

(9) 4:30: Keep SH across a track and follow a path along the edge of a hedgerow: do not bear right to climb the hill. Follow waymarks through a vineyard. Eventually, TL at a fork (no waymarks) and descend to cross a bridge over the railway. TR along the **B4008** near **Stonehouse**. Shortly afterwards, TL at a roundabout.

(10) 4:50: Cross a bridge over the **Stroudwater Canal**. Immediately afterwards, keep SH at a junction ('CW via Kings Stanley') to continue on **Stage 6**: alternatively, TL for the **Selsley Variant** (see below). Cross the **A419** at traffic lights and head S along **Ryeford Road South**. Shortly after crossing the **River Frome**, TL on a path. 10min later, bear right to skirt around a farm. Keep SH across the farm access lane and pick up a path through fields.

F 5:15: Arrive at **Middleyard**.

Selsley Variant (N-S)

(10) Head E along the **Stroudwater Canal** tow-path. For the **official route** of the CW, TR shortly after **Bridge Road**. However, for **our preferred route** (which we describe here), stay on the tow-path.

(1) 0:20: A few minutes later, reach a bridge near **Kitsch Coffee and Wine Bar** at **Ebley Wharf**: TR at the bridge to continue on the **Selsley Variant** or TL across the bridge to visit the bar. TL at a roundabout and pick up a path. Shortly afterwards, cross a bridge and keep SH on a path. Shortly after that, cross a stile and go through a tunnel. Then TL alongside the **A419**: you are now back on the CW official route. Shortly afterwards, cross the **A419** at traffic lights. Then keep SH, climbing on a path. Soon, go through a gate and climb a field.

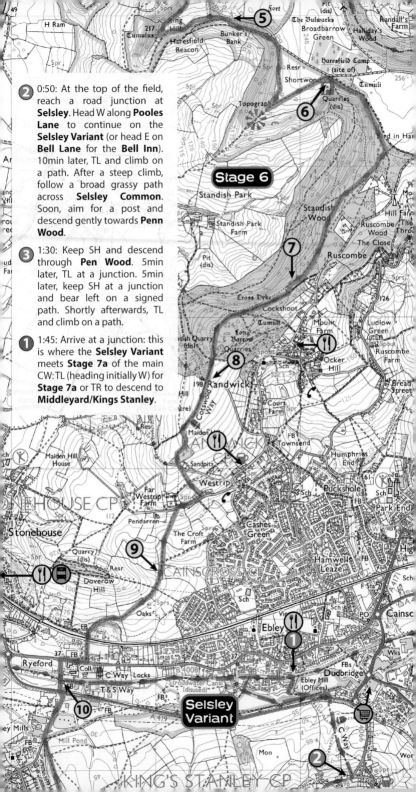

2 0:50: At the top of the field, reach a road junction at **Selsley**. Head W along **Pooles Lane** to continue on the **Selsley Variant** (or head E on **Bell Lane** for the **Bell Inn**). 10min later, TL and climb on a path. After a steep climb, follow a broad grassy path across **Selsley Common**. Soon, aim for a post and descend gently towards **Penn Wood**.

3 1:30: Keep SH and descend through **Pen Wood**. 5min later, TL at a junction. 5min later, keep SH at a junction and bear left on a signed path. Shortly afterwards, TL and climb on a path.

1 1:45: Arrive at a junction: this is where the **Selsley Variant** meets **Stage 7a** of the main CW: TL (heading initially W) for **Stage 7a** or TR to descend to **Middleyard/Kings Stanley**.

Stage 6

Selsley Variant

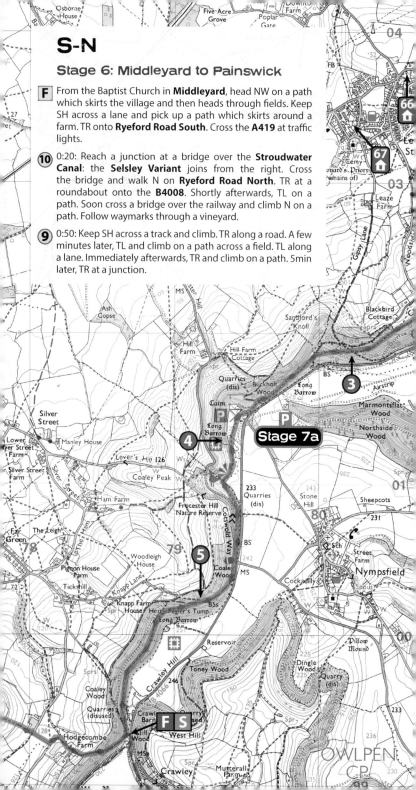

Stage 6: Middleyard to Painswick

F From the Baptist Church in **Middleyard**, head NW on a path which skirts the village and then heads through fields. Keep SH across a lane and pick up a path which skirts around a farm. TR onto **Ryeford Road South**. Cross the **A419** at traffic lights.

10 0:20: Reach a junction at a bridge over the **Stroudwater Canal**: the **Selsley Variant** joins from the right. Cross the bridge and walk N on **Ryeford Road North**. TR at a roundabout onto the **B4008**. Shortly afterwards, TL on a path. Soon cross a bridge over the railway and climb N on a path. Follow waymarks through a vineyard.

9 0:50: Keep SH across a track and climb. TR along a road. A few minutes later, TL and climb on a path across a field. TL along a lane. Immediately afterwards, TR and climb on a path. 5min later, TR at a junction.

8 1:40: 5-10min later, keep SH across a track.

7 2:05: TL on a path. Shortly, head NE at a junction. 20-25min later, TL at a junction.

6 2:40: TL through a car park and pick up a path heading SW. Turn sharp right at a **topograph**.

5 3:10: Bear right and climb steps. Then TL and head W along the edge of a beautiful ridge. Turn sharp right at **Haresfield Beacon** and descend.

4 3:25: TL down a road. Shortly afterwards, TR on a path. After a while, pass the **Cromwell Stone** which commemorates the raising of the siege of Gloucester in 1643. Soon, TR onto a path.

3 3:45: 5min later, head SE on a track through **Maitlands Wood**. Much later, TR and climb on a path. Soon, cross a road. Shortly afterwards, climb steps.

2 4:25: Head SE down **Rudge Hill**. At the **Edgemoor Inn**, TR alongside the **A4173**. Shortly afterwards, TL down a lane. Soon, TL on a path. Shortly, TR and go through a gate. Keep SH past a CW **stone marker**.

1 5:00: Shortly afterwards, go through a gate and continue NE. Just after passing **Washbrook Farm** (an old mill), TR at a junction. TR along **Edge Road**. A few minutes later, TL and head NE along **New Street**.

S 5:30: Arrive in the centre of **Painswick**.

5 Hetty Pegler's Tump

Uley Long Barrow is a Neolithic chambered burial mound, known locally as Hetty Pegler's Tump. It was excavated and reconstructed between 1854 and 1906. At least 15 skeletons have been found. Unlike many other burial mounds, you can explore the interior: bring a torch. It is a short distance OR.

7 Middleyard/ Wotton-under-Edge

his is one of the most beautiful parts of the CW. For long periods, you remain on the high escarpment, enjoying far-reaching panoramas and big skies. On a fine day, Stinchcombe Hill (above the town of Dursley) is a highlight with its sublime rural views. However, we think that the scenery at Nibley Knoll (where the splendid Tyndale Monument stands proud) is even better. Elsewhere too, the countryside is magnificent, including some arable farmland which looks particularly fine during the summer months, shortly before harvest. For the history buffs, there are two Neolithic burial mounds: one is right beside the CW and the other, which you can actually enter, is only 5-10min from the trail.

On Stage 7a, S-N trekkers have two options from ❶. The main route of the CW descends to Middleyard/King's Stanley: both villages have places to stay. However, if you have the time and energy, the Selsley Variant is the route to choose (see page 121): the variant re-joins the main CW at ❿ near Stonehouse. For N-S trekkers, the Selsley Variant is described on page 112.

Dursley (Stage 7b/7c) is a fairly large town and has plenty of shops for supplies. It also has many restaurants and the Old Spot Inn is one of the best real ale pubs on the CW. However, it is not the most attractive

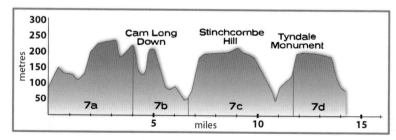

settlement on the trek and there is a dearth of good accommodation: as an alternative, you could stay in the Old Crown Inn in Uley (Stage 7a/7b; 0.6 miles OR). Further S, there are a few places to stay at North Nibley. Wotton-under-Edge is a lovely town with plenty of facilities, however, like Dursley, it only has a few accommodation options.

For S-N trekkers, Middleyard has a B&B. Alternatively, you could stay at Kings Stanley or Leonard Stanley, both of which are a short distance further NW. On the Selsley Variant, the Bell Inn is located in the village of Selsley and is a lovely place to stay/eat.

The section is generally well marked and navigation is straightforward. However, take care with route-finding in Pen Wood and Stanley Wood (both SW of Middleyard): there is a confusing array of paths. In poor conditions, you can avoid Stinchcombe Hill (Stage 7c) by using the Stinchcombe Hill Bypass, a short-cut between ① and ③ which saves about an hour.

		Time	Distance	Ascent N-S	Descent N-S
Stage 7a	Middleyard/ Uley exit	2:00(N-S) 1:45(S-N)	4.0miles 6.4km	787ft 240m	312ft 95m
Stage 7b	Uley exit/ Dursley	1:15(N-S) 1:45(S-N)	2.7miles 4.3km	295ft 90m	797ft 243m
Stage 7c	Dursley/ North Nibley	2:30	5.0miles 8.1km	732ft 223m	587ft 179m
Stage 7d	North Nibley/ Wotton-under-Edge	1:15	2.5miles 4.0km	282ft 86m	394ft 120m

Supplies/Water:

Dudbridge (Selsley Variant; 0.2 miles OR) - supermarket

Stroud (Selsley Variant; 1.7 miles OR) - supermarket, outdoor shops, pharmacy & ATM

Uley (Stage 7a/7b; 0.6 miles OR) - Uley Community Store (sandwiches, groceries & drinks)

Dursley (Stage 7b/7c) - supermarkets, shops, pharmacies & ATMs

S of ④ (Stage 7c) - water tap for hikers

Wotton-under-Edge (Stage 7d/8a) - supermarket, bakery, shops, pharmacy & ATM

Refreshments/Food:

Ebley Wharf (Selsley Variant) - Kitsch Coffee and Wine Bar

Stroud (Selsley Variant; 1.7 miles OR) - restaurants, pubs & cafés

Selsley (Selsley Variant) - the Bell Inn

Uley (Stage 7a/7b; 0.6 miles OR) - the Old Crown Inn; the Vestry Cafe

Dursley (Stage 7b/7c) - restaurants, pubs & cafés

North Nibley (Stage 7c/7d) - the Black Horse Inn; North Nibley Community Hub (drinks & cakes)

Wotton-under-Edge (Stage 7d/8a) - restaurants, pubs & cafés

Accommodation:

Middleyard (Stage 6/7a) - Valley Views B&B

Stroud (Selsley Variant; 1.7 miles OR) - Premier Inn Stroud hotel

Selsley (Selsley Variant) - the Bell Inn

Uley (Stage 7a/7b; 0.6 miles OR) - the Old Crown Inn

Dursley (Stage 7b/7c) - B&B & hotel

North Nibley (Stage 7c/7d) - the Black Horse Inn; Nibley Farm Campsite; Glamping pods at Hunt's Court Huts

Wotton-under-Edge (Stage 7d/8a) - the Swan Hotel; Hawks View B&B

The Tyndale Monument above North Nibley (Stage 7d)

Escape/Access:

Middleyard (Stage 6/7a) - bus

Ebley (Selsley Variant) - bus

Stroud (Selsley Variant; 1.7 miles OR) - bus; train

Selsley (Selsley Variant) - bus

Uley (Stage 7a/7b; 0.6 miles OR) - bus

Dursley (Stage 7b/7c) - bus; train (from Cam & Dursley station; 2.8miles OR)

Wotton-under-Edge (Stage 7d/8a) - bus

N-S

Stage 7a: Middleyard to Uley exit

S From the church in **Middleyard**, head SE along the road. Shortly afterwards, TR onto **Coombe Lane**. Shortly after that, TR at a junction. Soon continue on a path. Cross a lane and pass a cottage.

1 0:10: Reach a junction: the path arriving from the left is the **Selsley Variant**. TR and head initially W.

2 0:30: TL on a narrow path (easy to miss). 5-10min later, TL at a fork on a narrow path (no waymark). Shortly afterwards, the path splits: take either branch.

3 1:00: Keep SH at a junction and climb steeply. 10-15min later, TR at a fork. Shortly afterwards, TL and climb steps.

4 1:20: Reach **Nympsfield Long Barrow**, a Neolithic burial chamber (which was built around 3,800 BCE). Afterwards, keep SH along the edge of the escarpment, passing **Coaley Peak**. Follow signs carefully when you reach the **B4066**: the CW soon heads SW into **Coaley Wood**. However, if you wish to visit **Hetty Pegler's Tump** (see page 115), continue further S along the B4066 for 5min until you reach a path on the right which leads to this Neolithic burial mound.

5 1:40: Keep SH at a junction. 5min later, TL at a fork and climb.

F 2:00: Reach a junction beside the **B4066**. To start **Stage 7b**, TR and descend W on a path: alternatively, head S on another path to go to **Uley**.

Stage 7b: Uley exit to Dursley

S Descend W on a path. In **Hodgecombe Farm**, TR on a lane. A few minutes later, TL and cross a stile. Immediately afterwards, TR and walk up the side of a field. A few minutes later, keep SH and climb steeply up a grassy slope: enter the trees near the top. Soon bear left uphill on a path. Follow a path W along the crest of **Cam Long Down**: at the far end of the hill, descend on a path.

1 0:40: TL at a junction, still descending. Shortly afterwards, TL and descend along the side of a field. At the bottom of the slope, cross a lane and continue on a path.

2 0:55: TR and go through a gate. Then continue along the side of a field.

3 1:05: TR and descend on a lane. TL on **Long Street**.

F 1:15: Arrive in the centre of **Dursley**.

Beautiful pastures near Dursley (Stage 7b)

S-N

Stage 7b: Dursley to Uley exit

F From the centre of **Dursley**, head NE on **Long Street**. 5min later, before the Priory, TR on a lane.

3 0:10: TL and climb on a path.

2 0:25: Go through a gate and TL. Cross a lane and climb along the side of a field. At the end of the field, TR at a junction.

1 0:50: Shortly afterwards, head NE at a junction and climb. At the top of the slope, follow a path E along the crest of **Cam Long Down**. At the far end of the hill, head SE down a steep grassy slope. Soon after some buildings, TL. Head through **Hodgecombe Farm** and climb E on a path.

S 1:45: Reach a junction beside the **B4066**. To start **Stage 7a**, TL and head N on a path: alternatively, head S on another path to go to **Uley**.

Stage 7a: Uley exit to Middleyard

F From the junction beside the **B4066**, head N on a path: ignore the track to the W, running parallel to the path.

5 0:20: Keep SH at a junction. Follow the signs carefully when you reach the **B4066**: the CW soon heads N on a path. However, if you wish to visit **Hetty Pegler's Tump** (see page 115), head S along the **B4066** for 5min until you reach a path on the right which leads to this Neolithic burial mound. Head along the edge of the escarpment, passing **Coaley Peak**.

4 0:40: Pass **Nympsfield Long Barrow**, a Neolithic burial chamber which was built around 3,800 BCE.

3 1:00: Keep SH at a junction.

2 1:20: Keep SH at a junction.

1 1:35: Reach a junction. To continue on **Stage 7a**, descend N: alternatively, head E for the **Selsley Variant** (see below). Pass a cottage and cross a lane. Soon head through fields on a path.

S 1:45: TL on **Broad Street** and enter **Middleyard**.

Selsley Variant (S-N)

1 From the junction, head E on a path which snakes its way along the N fringes of **Pen Wood**. Shortly after the path bends left to head NE, TR on a path and climb (easy to miss).

3 0:20: Keep SH and emerge from the woods. Follow a broad grassy path N across **Selsley Common**. Soon descend steeply. At **Selsley**, TR along **Pooles Lane**.

2 0:50: 10min later, reach a road junction. To continue, TL and descend N on a path through a field: alternatively, head E on **Bell Lane** to head to the **Bell Inn**. At the bottom of the hill, cross the **A419** at traffic lights and then TL alongside the road. Soon, TR and go through a tunnel. Then cross a stile and head W on a path. Soon reach a junction: for the **official route** of the CW, keep SH. However, for **our preferred route** (described here), TR and cross a bridge: then TR at a roundabout and head N.

1 1:10: Shortly afterwards, reach a bridge over the **Stroudwater Canal** at **Ebley Wharf**. Cross the bridge if you wish to visit **Kitsch Coffee and Wine Bar** or TL and walk W along the tow-path to continue on the **Selsley Variant**. Just before **Bridge Road**, the official route of the CW joins from the left.

10 1:30: TR and cross a bridge over the **Stroudwater Canal** to start **Stage 6**.

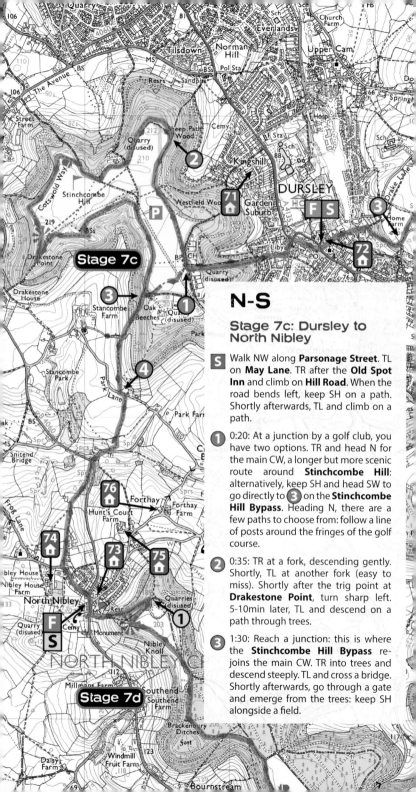

N-S

Stage 7c: Dursley to North Nibley

S Walk NW along **Parsonage Street**. TL on **May Lane**. TR after the **Old Spot Inn** and climb on **Hill Road**. When the road bends left, keep SH on a path. Shortly afterwards, TL and climb on a path.

1 0:20: At a junction by a golf club, you have two options. TR and head N for the main CW, a longer but more scenic route around **Stinchcombe Hill**: alternatively, keep SH and head SW to go directly to **3** on the **Stinchcombe Hill Bypass**. Heading N, there are a few paths to choose from: follow a line of posts around the fringes of the golf course.

2 0:35: TR at a fork, descending gently. Shortly, TL at another fork (easy to miss). Shortly after the trig point at **Drakestone Point**, turn sharp left. 5-10min later, TL and descend on a path through trees.

3 1:30: Reach a junction: this is where the **Stinchcombe Hill Bypass** rejoins the main CW. TR into trees and descend steeply. TL and cross a bridge. Shortly afterwards, go through a gate and emerge from the trees: keep SH alongside a field.

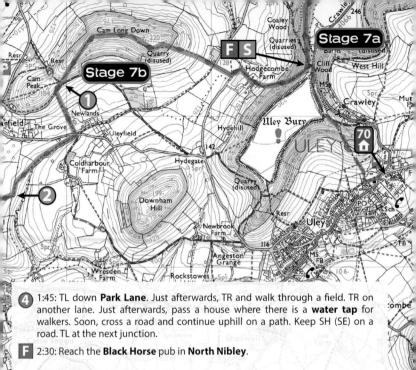

4 1:45: TL down **Park Lane**. Just afterwards, TR and walk through a field. TR on another lane. Just afterwards, pass a house where there is a **water tap** for walkers. Soon, cross a road and continue uphill on a path. Keep SH (SE) on a road. TL at the next junction.

F 2:30: Reach the **Black Horse** pub in **North Nibley**.

S-N

Stage 7c: North Nibley to Dursley

F From **North Nibley**, head NW on a road known as '**The Street**'. After 5min, TR and descend on a path. Keep SH across a road and continue on a lane. Pass a house where there is a **water tap** for walkers. Just afterwards, TL on a path and climb.

4 0:45: TL along **Park Lane**. Just afterwards, TR and continue climbing.

3 1:10: At a junction, you have two options. Head N for the main CW, a longer but more scenic route around **Stinchcombe Hill**: alternatively, head NE to go directly to **1** on the **Stinchcombe Hill Bypass**. Heading N, follow a path around the edges of the hill. Turn sharp right at **Drakestone Point**. Shortly afterwards, pass a trig point.

2 2:00: Keep SH (S) at two junctions.

1 2:15: Just after the **golf clubhouse**, TL and descend on a path through trees. Keep SH down a road. After the **Old Spot Inn**, TL onto **May Lane**.

S 2:30: Arrive in the centre of Dursley.

1 Tyndale Monument

The Tyndale Monument was built in 1866 on Nibley Knoll, overlooking the village of North Nibley. It commemorates the writer, William Tyndale, who may have been born nearby. Tyndale translated the New Testament into English in 1525. In 1536, he was martyred in Flanders. The tower is 34m tall and there is a staircase inside: the monument is often open to the public.

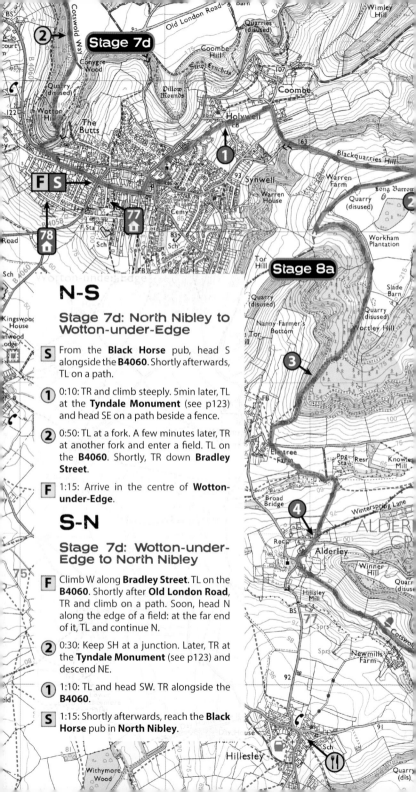

N-S

Stage 7d: North Nibley to Wotton-under-Edge

S From the **Black Horse** pub, head S alongside the **B4060**. Shortly afterwards, TL on a path.

1 0:10: TR and climb steeply. 5min later, TL at the **Tyndale Monument** (see p123) and head SE on a path beside a fence.

2 0:50: TL at a fork. A few minutes later, TR at another fork and enter a field. TL on the **B4060**. Shortly, TR down **Bradley Street**.

F 1:15: Arrive in the centre of **Wotton-under-Edge**.

S-N

Stage 7d: Wotton-under-Edge to North Nibley

F Climb W along **Bradley Street**. TL on the **B4060**. Shortly after **Old London Road**, TR and climb on a path. Soon, head N along the edge of a field: at the far end of it, TL and continue N.

2 0:30: Keep SH at a junction. Later, TR at the **Tyndale Monument** (see p123) and descend NE.

1 1:10: TL and head SW. TR alongside the **B4060**.

S 1:15: Shortly afterwards, reach the **Black Horse** pub in **North Nibley**.

Stage 8a

The view from Coaley Peak
(Stage 7a)

Monarch's Way
Knight's Grove
Hammouth Hill
Kilcott Mill
Mill Pond
5
74

Wotton-under-Edge/ Old Sodbury

A beautiful walk on undulating paths along the Cotswold Escarpment, passing pastures, woods and arable fields. Although the scenery is sometimes less dramatic than that further N, there are still plenty of fabulous views to enjoy and the wild-flowers in spring are wonderful. Magnificent sections of dry-stone walling, Iron Age hill-forts and historic monuments all add to the experience too.

Although the village of Hawkesbury Upton is a short distance OR, it is an attractive place to stop for lunch: it has two pubs, one of which also offers

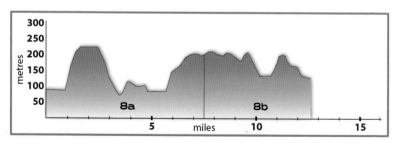

B&B. There are more accommodation options at Old Sodbury, although some of them are OR: campers will be pleased to learn that there is a nearby campsite (best accessed from ④).

For S-N trekkers, Wotton-under Edge is a lovely town with plenty of facilities, however, it only has a few accommodation options.

The section is well marked and navigation is straightforward.

		Time	Distance	Ascent N-S	Descent N-S
Stage 8a	Wotton-under-Edge/ Hawkesbury Upton	4:00(N-S) 3:45(S-N)	7.5miles 12.0km	925ft 282m	584ft 178m
Stage 8b	Hawkesbury Upton/ Old Sodbury	2:30(N-S) 2:45(S-N)	5.3miles 8.5km	367ft 112m	591ft 180m

Supplies/Water:

Wotton-under-Edge (Stage 7d/8a) - supermarket, bakery, shops, pharmacy & ATM

Hawkesbury Upton (Stage 8a/8b; 0.3 miles OR) - Hawkesbury Stores village shop (bread & groceries)

Old Sodbury (Stage 8b/9a) - service station (sandwiches, drinks & snacks)

Refreshments/Food:

Wotton-under-Edge (Stage 7d/8a) - restaurants, pubs & cafés

Hillesley (Stage 8a; 0.6 miles OR) - the Fleece Inn

Hawkesbury Upton (Stage 8a/8b; 0.3 miles OR) - the Fox Inn; the Beaufort Arms

Old Sodbury (Stage 8b/9a) - the Dog Inn; Cross Hands Hotel (0.8 miles OR); the Bell Inn (1 mile OR)

Accommodation:

Wotton-under-Edge (Stage 7d/8a) - the Swan Hotel; Hawks View B&B

Hawkesbury Upton (Stage 8a/8b; 0.3 miles OR) - the Fox Inn

Cotswold Meadow Camping (Stage 8b; 0.7 miles OR)

Old Sodbury (Stage 8b/9a) - B&Bs, pubs & hotel

Escape/Access:

Wotton-under-Edge (Stage 7d/8a) - bus

Alderley (Stage 8a) - bus

Hawkesbury Upton (Stage 8a/8b; 0.3 miles OR) - bus

Horton (Stage 8b) - bus

Old Sodbury (Stage 8b/9a) - bus

Vast arable fields near
Hawkesbury Upton (Stage 8a)

⑧ Somerset Monument

The Somerset Monument near Hawkesbury Upton was erected in 1846 in memory of General Lord Robert Somerset (1776-1842), a British soldier who fought at the Battle of Waterloo. The stone tower is more than 30m high and has a viewing platform at the top.

Stage 8a

Stage 8b

⑧ The Somerset Monument (Stage 8a)

N-S

Stage 8a: Wotton-under-Edge to Hawkesbury Upton

S Head N on **Church Street**: at the end of it, cross a road and then TR on a path. Soon, pass through the grounds of the **Church of St Mary the Virgin**. Afterwards, TR along a road. Shortly, TR on **Valley Road**. Immediately afterwards, TL at a fork.

1 0:20: TR on a lane beside a picnic area. Just afterwards, TL on a path. 5min later, TR along a lane which soon climbs. A few minutes later, TL at a junction. Shortly afterwards, TR and climb steeply on a path. TL onto another lane and continue climbing.

2 1:00: TR at a junction. Just afterwards, TR on a track.

3 1:40: Keep SH and descend on a rocky path. 10min later, TL on a track. Soon, cross a lane and head through a field.

4 2:10: At **Alderley**, TR onto a lane. Shortly afterwards, cross a road and keep SH on another road. At a junction, turn sharp left on another road. Shortly afterwards, keep SH on a path.

5 2:45: TR onto a track. A few minutes later, TL onto a lane.

6 3:10: TR on a muddy path.

7 3:30: TL and climb along the side of a field. Soon TR at a junction.

8 3:55: At the **Somerset Monument** (see box), TL along a road.

F 4:00: Just NW of **Hawkesbury Upton**, reach a junction.

S-N

Stage 8a: Hawkesbury Upton to Wotton-under-Edge

F From the junction at **Hawkesbury Upton**, head NW on a road.

8 0:05: Just before the **Somerset Monument** (see box), TR onto a path. 15mins later, TL and head N along the side of a field.

7 0:25: TR on a path. After 10min, TR on a track.

6 0:40: TL on a lane. At a junction, TR onto a track.

5 1:05: Shortly afterwards, TL on a path. When you reach a road junction, TR.

4 1:40: At **Alderley**, cross a road junction and keep SH on a lane. Shortly afterwards, TL at a junction. At **Wortley**, cross a lane and climb on a track. Shortly afterwards, TR and climb on a path.

3 2:15: Keep SH, climbing NE.

2 3:00: TL at a junction and descend W on a lane. After a while, TR and descend on a path. Head N on **Coombe Lane**. A few minutes later, TL on a path.

1 3:30: 5min later, TR on a lane. Just afterwards, TL on a path. Keep SH and head SW on **Valley Road**. TL onto the **B4058**. TL through the grounds of the **Church of St Mary the Virgin**. TL at a roundabout with a war memorial and head SW along **Church Street**. TR on **Long Street**.

S 3:45: Arrive in the centre of **Wotton-under-Edge**.

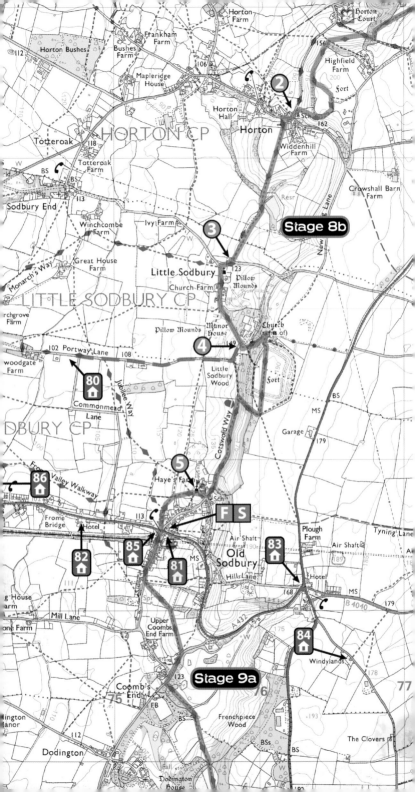

Stage 8b

Stage 9a

N-S

Stage 8b: Hawkesbury Upton to Old Sodbury

S From the junction, head SW on a lane beside a pond. Soon, TL on a path.

1 0:45: TR at a fork. Later, head diagonally through **Horton Camp hill-fort** (Iron Age): afterwards, TR and descend past a little **tower** (built in 2000 as a millennium project to provide nesting places for swallows and owls).

2 1:15: At the bottom of the slope, TL down a road. Shortly afterwards, TR at a junction at the village of **Horton**. Shortly, TL and head S on a path.

3 1:35: Cross a stile in the corner of a field (hard to spot). Shortly afterwards, TR down a minor road. Soon, TL at a junction in **Little Sodbury**.

4 1:50: TL and climb on a path: alternatively continue along **Portway Lane** to head to **Cotswold Meadow Camping**. Soon, go through a gate and TL at a junction. After a short climb, follow the path through a large **hill-fort**: afterwards, go through a gate, TR and descend. At the bottom of the slope, TL and head across the top of a field.

5 2:25: Head through the yard of the **Church of St John the Baptist**. Afterwards, descend a grassy slope. Go through a farm.

F 2:30: Arrive in **Old Sodbury**.

S-N

Stage 8b: Old Sodbury to Hawkesbury Upton

F Head N on a lane through a farm. Afterwards, climb on a path.

5 0:10: Head through the yard of the **Church of St John the Baptist**. Afterwards, head N on a path. 10-15min later, TR and climb. After a short climb, TL and follow a path through a large **hill-fort**: at the other side of it, follow a path which soon descends W.

4 0:50: TR at a junction and head NW on a lane: alternatively, TL along **Portway Lane** to head to **Cotswold Meadow Camping**. TR at a junction in **Little Sodbury**.

3 1:05: Shortly afterwards, TL. Cross a stile and head N on a path. At **Horton**, TR on a road. Shortly afterwards, TL at a junction.

2 1:30: TR and climb on a path. Pass a little **tower** (built in 2000 as a millennium project to provide nesting places for swallows and owls). Soon afterwards, TL and head diagonally through **Horton Camp hill-fort** (Iron Age).

1 2:05: Keep SH at a junction.

S 2:45: Just NW of **Hawkesbury Upton**, reach a junction.

Church of St John the Baptist at Old Sodbury (Stage 8b)

9 Old Sodbury/Cold Ashton

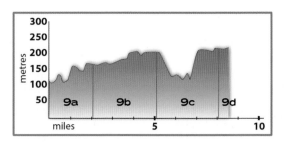

For N-S trekkers the end of the CW is now in sight and the scenery becomes less dramatic than that on the high, steep parts of the Cotswold Escarpment further N. However, this is still beautiful countryside with glorious rolling pastures, striking fields of rapeseed (with its bright yellow blossom), lovely villages and some of the finest dry-stone walls in the region. It is lovely to take your time, stopping at one of the pubs just OR. For S-N trekkers, things will be 'hotting up' with slightly better scenery than the previous section: the views will continue to improve incrementally over the next few days.

If you have time, be sure to visit the magnificent Dryham Park which will be a highlight of the day. Dryham Park has been occupied since ancient times but the house and gardens which you see today date from the end of the 17th century. They were commissioned by William Blathwayt (c.1649-1717): as a leading colonial administrator, he was able to source, for the house, the finest materials from across the globe including marble, walnut, cedar and silk. After Blathwayt's death, his heirs, experiencing financial difficulties, allowed the house to fall into disrepair. In 1844, Lieutenant Colonel George Blathwayt inherited Dryham and he embarked on a programme of repair and modernisation. In 1956, the Ministry of Works purchased the house and it was subsequently transferred to the National Trust. In 1961, after extensive repairs, the house was opened to the public. The park was purchased in 1976. The National Trust has since carried

out extensive work to restore parts of the house and gardens to display them as they were originally designed by William Blathwayt. Visitors can currently view a range of 17th-century showrooms (entrance fee; free for National Trust members).

Unfortunately, Section 9 is in the midst of an accommodation crisis. Tormarton (Stage 9a/9b) is a lovely village and there used to be a variety of B&Bs, but only one of them has survived the Covid epidemic. Fortunately, you can still stay at the village pub or the nearby hotel. At Cold Ashton too (Stage 9d/10), much accommodation has closed and, at the date of press, there was nowhere to stay within the village itself: there are still a few good options OR and there is B&B accommodation at Hill Farm (which is actually beside the route of Stage 10, one mile from Cold Ashton). Both the pub and café in Cold Ashton have closed too so there is nowhere serving meals within the village. Hill Farm does serve evening meals for guests but, if you cannot secure a booking there, consider getting a taxi to Marshfield (2.2 miles E of Cold Aston) to stay/eat at the Catherine Wheel pub. The Crown pub at Tolldown (Stage 9b/9c; 0.4 miles OR) is also a great place to spend the night. And there are two B&Bs at Pennsylvania (Stage 9c/9d).

The section is well marked and navigation is straightforward.

		Time	Distance	Ascent N-S	Descent N-S
Stage 9a	Old Sodbury/ Tormarton	1:00(N-S) 0:45(S-N)	2.1miles 3.4km	236ft 72m	92ft 28m
Stage 9b	Tormarton/ Tolldown exit	1:30	3.0miles 4.8km	131ft 40m	39ft 12m
Stage 9c	Tolldown exit/ Pennsylvania	1:30	3.0miles 4.8km	262ft 80m	266ft 81m
Stage 9d	Pennsylvania/ Cold Ashton	0:15	0.4miles 0.7km	115ft 35m	66ft 20m

Supplies/Water:

Old Sodbury (Stage 8b/9a) - service station (sandwiches, drinks & snacks)

Pennsylvania (Stage 9c/9d) - service station (sandwiches, drinks & snacks)

Refreshments/Food:

Old Sodbury (Stage 8b/9a) - the Dog Inn; Cross Hands Hotel (0.8 miles OR); the Bell Inn (1 mile OR)

Tormarton (Stage 9a/9b) - the Major's Retreat; Compass Inn

Tolldown (Stage 9b/9c; 0.4 miles OR) - the Crown pub

Hinton (Stage 9b/9c; 0.8 miles OR) - the Bull pub

Marshfield (Stage 9c/9d/10; 2.2 miles OR) - the Catherine Wheel pub

A fabulous dry-stone wall on Stage 9b

Accommodation:

Old Sodbury (Stage 8b/9a) - B&Bs, pubs & hotel

Tormarton (Stage 9a/9b) - the Major's Retreat; Compass Inn; Noades House B&B

Tolldown (Stage 9b/9c; 0.4 miles OR) - the Crown pub

Pennsylvania (Stage 9c/9d) - B&Bs

Cold Ashton (Stage 9d/10) - B&Bs (all OR)

Marshfield (Stage 9c/9d/10; 2.2 miles OR) - the Catherine Wheel pub

Escape/Access:

Old Sodbury (Stage 8b/9a) - bus

Cold Ashton (Stage 9d/10) - bus

N-S

Stage 9a: Old Sodbury to Tormarton

S From the **Dog Inn**, head S on **Chapel Lane**. After 5min, ignore a footpath on the left. Immediately afterwards, TL through a gate. Immediately after that, TR at a fork. TR down a road. 5min later, TL on a path.

1 0:50: Keep SH across the busy **A46** and pick up a path heading SE. TL onto a road at the village of **Tormarton**. Shortly afterwards, head E on a path. Soon TR at the **Church of St Mary Magdalene**.

F 1:00: Arrive at the **Major's Retreat** pub.

Stage 9b: Tormarton to Tolldown exit

S From the **Major's Retreat** pub, head SE along **High Street**. Follow the road across a bridge over the **M4** motorway: afterwards, take care as there is no footpath.

1 0:10: TR on a minor road. 5min later, TL through a farmyard.

2 0:50: Arrive at the **A46**: cross it at a nearby traffic island. Then head N on an access road. A few minutes later, TL on a path through trees.

F 1:30: Arrive at a road: keep SH across it to start **Stage 9c** or TL along it for **Tolldown**.

Stage 9c: Tolldown exit to Pennsylvania

S Bear left across the road and continue S on a lane. 5min later, TR into a field.

1 0:25: At the village of **Dryham**, TL along a lane. Shortly afterwards, pass **Dryham Park** (see page 134).

2 0:30: TL at a road junction. Soon, TR on a path.

3 0:50: When the path bends right near a pond, TL through a field. Soon, enter **Dryham Wood**: look out for the message box where hikers can jot down their musings for others to read.

4 1:15: Cross a road and TL on a path behind a hedgerow.

F 1:30: Reach the **A46** at **Pennsylvania**.

S-N

Stage 9c: Pennsylvania to Tolldown exit

F From the **A46** at **Pennsylvania**, head NW on a path.

4 0:10: Cross a road and continue NW. Soon, enter **Dryham Wood**: look out for the message box where hikers can jot down their musings for others to read.

3 0:30: Shortly after a pond, keep SH at a junction, heading N. When you reach a road, TL.

2 0:50: TR at a road junction. Shortly afterwards, pass **Dryham Park** (see page 134).

1 0:55: TR and climb on a path. TL on a lane.

S 1:30: Arrive at a road: cross it to start **Stage 9b** or TR along it for **Tolldown**.

Stage 9c

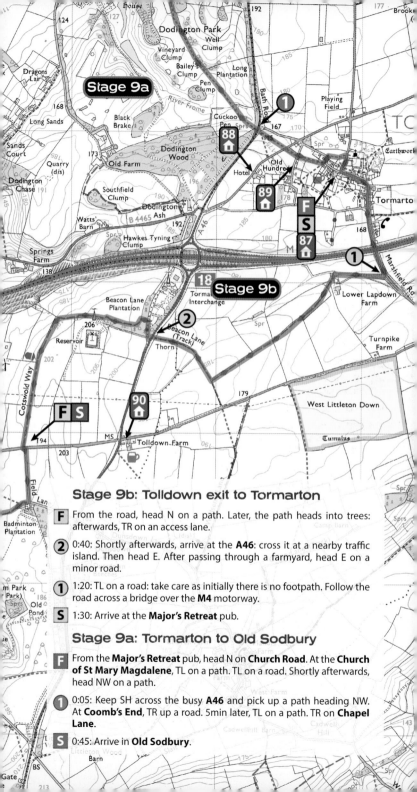

Stage 9b: Tolldown exit to Tormarton

F From the road, head N on a path. Later, the path heads into trees: afterwards, TR on an access lane.

2 0:40: Shortly afterwards, arrive at the **A46**: cross it at a nearby traffic island. Then head E. After passing through a farmyard, head E on a minor road.

1 1:20: TL on a road: take care as initially there is no footpath. Follow the road across a bridge over the **M4** motorway.

S 1:30: Arrive at the **Major's Retreat** pub.

Stage 9a: Tormarton to Old Sodbury

F From the **Major's Retreat** pub, head N on **Church Road**. At the **Church of St Mary Magdalene**, TL on a path. TL on a road. Shortly afterwards, head NW on a path.

1 0:05: Keep SH across the busy **A46** and pick up a path heading NW. At **Coomb's End**, TR up a road. 5min later, TL on a path. TR on **Chapel Lane**.

S 0:45: Arrive in **Old Sodbury**.

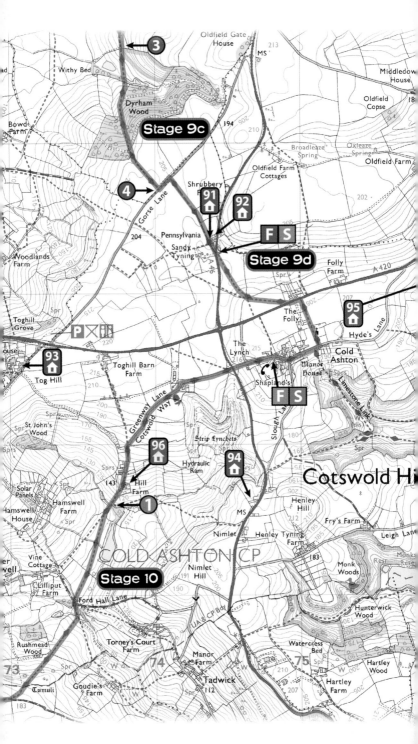

The Norman church at Old Sodbury is more than 900 years old (Stage 8b/9a)

N-S

Stage 9d: Pennsylvania to Cold Ashton

S From the **A46** at **Pennsylvania**, head SE on a path through a field. TL alongside a road. Shortly afterwards, TR and continue beside a wall. Soon, pass through a churchyard. Shortly afterwards, TR along **Hyde's Lane**.

F 0:15: Reach the **Parish Hall** in **Cold Ashton**.

S-N

Stage 9d: Cold Ashton to Pennsylvania

F Head E along **Hyde's Lane** in **Cold Ashton**. A few minutes later, TL on a path. Soon, pass through a churchyard. TL alongside a road. Shortly afterwards, TR and head through fields.

S 0:15: Reach the **A46** at **Pennsylvania**.

10 Cold Ashton/Bath

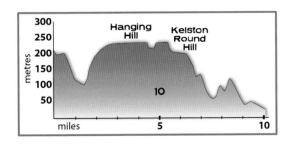

I f you are travelling N-S, rolling hills and lovely farmland accompany you all the way to the historic City of Bath where your journey will end. And what a place to finish! Bath is one of England's finest attractions and provides a wonderful climax to an amazing trek. The city is famous for its Roman Baths, an exquisite abbey and the incredible Georgian architecture of its buildings including one of the most famous structures in the country, the magnificent Royal Crescent (which is along the route of the CW). There are surely few better places to spend a day or two at the end of a long walk and it is fair to say that many people walk N-S for this very reason. For further information on Bath, see page 150.

S-N trekkers, of course, will instead be starting their journey in Bath but there is nothing wrong with that: the CW is fortunate enough to have Chipping Camden, one of England's best-preserved market towns, at its northern extremity and that is also a fabulous place to end the trek.

Because Bath is undoubtedly the highlight of the day, many N-S trekkers rush the rest of Section 10 in their eagerness to get there. That is a shame because there is still plenty to catch the eye, including the wonderful views over Bath as you approach/leave the city. The route also passes Lansdown

which hosted one of the most famous battles of the English Civil War. The site has barely changed in the intervening years except for the erection of the information boards and flags that now adorn it.

The CW starts/finishes at a CW marker stone on the ground in front of Bath Abbey, which mirrors the marker stone at the start/finish of the trail in Chipping Campden: like its sister stone, the Bath stone is carved with the names of places along the trek, however, the inscription around the outer ring of the Bath stone differs. It bears a verse from the Old Testament: 'Stand ye in the ways and see, ask for the old paths, where is the good way, and walk therein, and ye shall find rest for your souls' (Jeremiah 6:16).

For S-N trekkers the section finishes at Cold Ashton (Stage 9d/10): unfortunately, much accommodation has closed and, at the date of press, there was nowhere to stay within the village itself. There are still a few good options OR and there is B&B accommodation at Hill Farm (which is along the route of Stage 10, one mile before Cold Ashton). Both the pub and café in Cold Ashton have closed too so there is nowhere serving meals within the village. Hill Farm does serve evening meals for guests but, if you cannot get a booking there, consider getting a taxi to Marshfield (2.2 miles E of Cold Aston) to stay/eat at the Catherine Wheel pub.

The section is generally well marked, however, in Bath, the markings are more difficult to follow: look out for small black and gold waymarks on lampposts.

		Time	Distance	Ascent N-S	Descent N-S
Stage 10	Cold Ashton/ Bath	5:00 (N-S) 5:30 (S-N)	10.1miles 16.2km	787ft 240m	1398ft 426m

Supplies/Water:

Weston (Stage 10) - supermarket, pharmacy & ATM

Bath (Stage 10) - supermarkets, outdoor shops, pharmacies & ATMs

Refreshments/Food:

Marshfield (Stage 9d/10; 2.2 miles OR) - the Catherine Wheel pub

Lansdown (Stage 10; 0.8 mile OR) - the Charlcombe Inn

Weston (Stage 10) - the Old Crown pub; Western Bistro; cafés; take-away restaurants

Bath (Stage 10) - restaurants, pubs, tea rooms & cafés

Accommodation:

Cold Ashton (Stage 9d/10) - B&Bs (all OR)

Marshfield (Stage 9d/10; 2.2 miles OR) - the Catherine Wheel pub

Hill Farm B&B (Stage 10; 1 mile SW of Cold Ashton)

Lansdown (Stage 10; 0.8 mile OR) - the Charlcombe Inn

Bath (Stage 10) - hostels, B&Bs & hotels

Escape/Access:

Cold Ashton (Stage 9d/10) - bus

Weston (Stage 10) - bus

Bath (Stage 10) - bus; train

*The site of the Battle of Lansdown
(Stage 10)*

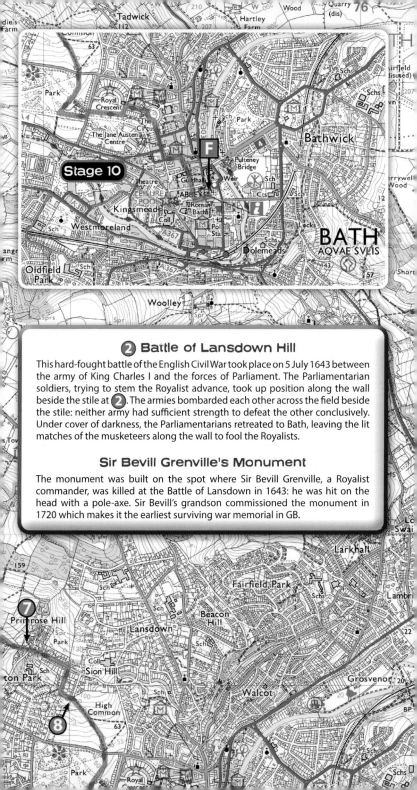

② Battle of Lansdown Hill

This hard-fought battle of the English Civil War took place on 5 July 1643 between the army of King Charles I and the forces of Parliament. The Parliamentarian soldiers, trying to stem the Royalist advance, took up position along the wall beside the stile at ②. The armies bombarded each other across the field beside the stile: neither army had sufficient strength to defeat the other conclusively. Under cover of darkness, the Parliamentarians retreated to Bath, leaving the lit matches of the musketeers along the wall to fool the Royalists.

Sir Bevill Grenville's Monument

The monument was built on the spot where Sir Bevill Grenville, a Royalist commander, was killed at the Battle of Lansdown in 1643: he was hit on the head with a pole-axe. Sir Bevill's grandson commissioned the monument in 1720 which makes it the earliest surviving war memorial in GB.

N-S

Stage 10: Cold Ashton to Bath

S From the **Parish Hall** in **Cold Ashton**, continue W along the road. At a junction, bear left and descend. Soon cross the **A46** and keep SH on a lane.

1 0:25: Shortly after **Hill Farm B&B**, TR on a path. TL down a lane. Soon TR and climb on a path through a field.

2 1:20: Cross a stile with an orange flag. This is the site of the **Battle of Lansdown** (see page 147). Later, pass **Sir Bevill Grenville's Monument** (see page 147). A few minutes later, cross a road and keep SH on a path. Shortly afterwards, TR on a lane. Soon, TR onto a path.

3 1:55: TL at the trig point on **Hanging Hill** and follow a path beside a dry-stone wall. Keep SH alongside a golf course: watch out for golf balls.

4 2:15: TR at a junction. At **Little Down**, you can just make out the contours of an Iron Age hill-fort.

5 3:00: Go through a tall gate. Then TL and go through another gate: immediately afterwards, TR.

6 3:35: Keep SH down a lane. Shortly afterwards, TR on a path. Keep SH across playing fields: at the other side, TL down **Penn Hill Road** into **Weston**. Cross the road at a zebra crossing and TR on **High Street**. Soon, keep SH through an alley. Just after a Tesco supermarket, bear left and climb. Pass to the right of a church and then TL up **Church Road**. Keep SH across **Purlewent Drive**. Soon there are good views of Bath.

7 4:15: After climbing through an alley, cross a road and continue uphill on the other side. Soon, keep SH on **Summerhill Road**. A few minutes later, TR down **Sion Hill**.

8 4:25: TR on a path. Soon, keep SH at a fork. Cross **Weston Road** and head S along the side of **Royal Victoria Park**. At the far side of the park, TL at a junction, passing the **Victoria Majority Monument**. At the next junction, TL. Shortly afterwards, TR on a path just below the famous **Royal Crescent**: TL at the far side of the Crescent. Then TR onto Brock Street. TR at the Circus and head S down **Gay Street**. TL on **Wood Street**. Keep SH along **Quiet Street**. TR along **New Bond Street**: shortly afterwards, keep SH onto **Burton Street**. Keep SH along **Union Street**. Keep SH on **Stall Street**.

F 5:00: Shortly afterwards, TL to arrive at **Bath Abbey** and the **Roman Baths**. Congratulations! You have completed the CW.

S-N

Stage 10: Bath to Cold Ashton

F From **Bath Abbey/Roman Baths**, head N on **Stall Street**. Shortly afterwards, keep SH onto **Burton Street**. Keep SH onto **New Bond Street**. Shortly afterwards, TL onto **Quiet Street**. Keep SH along **Wood Street**. TR into **Queen Square**. Keep SH up **Gay Street**. Head along the left side of **the Circus**. Then TL onto **Brock Street**. TL just before the famous **Royal Crescent**: shortly afterwards, TR on a path just below it. TL at the far side of the Crescent. Shortly afterwards, TR at a junction, passing the **Victoria Majority Monument**. Soon, TR and head N along the side of **Royal Victoria Park**. At the far side of the park, cross **Weston Road** and head N on a path across the **High Common**.

8 0:40: TL on **Sion Hill**. TL on **Summerhill Road**.

7 0:55: Cross a road and continue downhill on the other side. Later, keep SH across **Purlewent Drive** and descend on **Church Road** into **Weston**. At a junction, TR

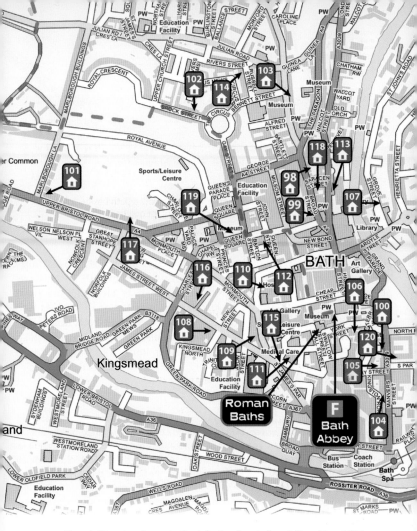

onto **Church Street** and pass to the left of a church. Bear left and head NW on **High Street**. Cross a road at a zebra crossing and head SW up **Penn Hill Road**. TR into **Weston Recreational Ground**: pick up a path on the far side of it and climb.

6 1:40: Keep SH up a lane. Shortly afterwards, keep SH climbing on a path.

5 2:25: TL and go through a gate. Then TR and go through a tall gate. At **Little Down**, you can just make out the contours of an **Iron Age hill-fort**.

4 3:10: TL at a junction. Keep SH alongside a golf course: watch out for golf balls.

3 3:35: TR at the trig point on **Hanging Hill**. After a while, TL on a lane. Cross a road and head NE on a path. Pass **Sir Bevill Grenville's Monument** (see page 147). Pass the site of the **Battle of Lansdown** (see page 147).

2 4:10: Cross a stile with an orange flag. Then bear left and descend. After descending through fields, TL on a lane. Soon TR on a path.

1 5:00: Keep SH at a junction and climb NE. **Pass Hill Farm B&B**. Cross the **A46** and keep SH on a lane. Keep SH at a junction.

S 5:25: Reach the **Parish Hall** in **Cold Ashton**.

Exploring Bath

The Royal Crescent in Bath

One of the joys of the CW is that it provides the perfect opportunity to stay a night or two in the well-preserved City of Bath. This historic place is packed with fascinating sights and it is arguably the most beautiful and interesting city on any of England's National Trails. As well as incredible attractions such as the Roman Baths and Bath Abbey, the city is full of excellent pubs, restaurants, hotels, B&Bs and hostels which cater for all budgets and tastes. For further information on Bath, see **www.visitbath.co.uk**.

History

Bath has its origins in the 1st century CE when the Romans founded the small town of Aquae Sulis (which means 'waters of Sulis'). Around 60 CE, they began to build a temple and baths in the town to take advantage of the location's natural hot springs. Over time, the facilities were built up into a major bath complex. After the collapse of the Roman Empire, the baths fell into disrepair. By the 9th century, the baths and the old Roman street plan were lost and the town was freshly laid out by King Alfred the Great. During the early and late Middle Ages, the restorative and healing effects of the hot spring water were recognised and the area around the natural springs was redeveloped several times.

In the 16th century, the baths were improved and many aristocrats visited the city. During the Georgian era (1714-1830), the number of visitors increased dramatically and new buildings were required to accommodate them. The architect John Wood the Elder, and his son (John Wood the Younger), laid out streets of new quarters with identical façades using a creamy-gold limestone: between them, they were responsible for a large proportion of Bath's most celebrated structures including the sublime Royal Crescent which was designed by Wood the Younger. Many of the buildings were badly damaged by bombs during WW2 but most have since been restored. In 1987, the city became a UNESCO World Heritage Site.

What to see

The Roman Baths are the reason Bath got its name and are the city's most important attraction. They were not rediscovered until the late 19th century and re-opened to the public in 1897. In fact, the complex is one of the best-preserved Roman sites in the world and has four main features:

- ▶ **The Sacred Spring** at the heart of the site from which 1.17 million litres of water rise daily

- ▶ **The Roman Temple** built to worship the goddess Sulis Minerva

- ▶ **The Roman Baths** themselves including heated rooms, plunge pools and the famous Great Bath

- ▶ **The Museum** housing the thousands of important finds from the site including Minerva's Head (one of the best-known objects from Roman Britain)

You can also visit the Georgian Pump Room and sample the spring water. For further information and tickets, see **www.romanbaths.co.uk**.

Bath Abbey, where the CW starts/finishes, is one of the most beautiful churches in England. The current structure dates from the end of the 15th century when it replaced a Norman church that had fallen into disrepair. Not long afterwards, in 1539, it was shut down by Henry VIII and left to decay. In 1560, the ruins were given to the City of Bath to use as its parish church. Restoration works were completed in 1620. In the 19th century, the abbey was again restored with some major changes to its design. For further information and visiting times, see **www.bathabbey.org**.

The Royal Crescent is Bath's best-known architectural delight. It is a huge curved terrace of 30 uniform houses which was built in the 18th century to the design of John Wood the Younger. The creamy-gold limestone façade was constructed in the Palladian style. Today, No.1 Royal Crescent is a Georgian town-house museum: for tickets and further information, see **www.no1royalcrescent.org.uk**.

Lansdown Crescent is the less famous, but equally splendid, sister of the Royal Crescent. It is located on an elevated site to the N of the city and is clearly visible from the CW (on the approach to Bath).

The Bath Assembly Rooms were completed in 1771. They were designed by John Wood the Younger as a venue for balls and concerts. You can visit each of the four beautiful rooms. For further information, **see www.nationaltrust.org.uk**.

The Museum of Bath Architecture is the place to visit if you really want to immerse yourself in the city's Georgian past. The exhibits explain how and why Bath was transformed from a small medieval town into a showcase for Georgian architecture. The collection includes maps, models, designs and drawings. For further information, see **www.museumofbatharchitecture.org.uk**.

The Herschel Museum of Astronomy is located in a well-preserved Georgian town-house and is the former home of the Herschels, astronomers who discovered the planet Uranus in 1781. It is worth visiting even if astronomy is not your bag: the rooms have been fully restored complete with period furniture. For further information, see **www.herschelmuseum.org.uk**.

The Holburne Museum was Bath's first public art museum and is housed in a Grade 1 listed building. It includes works by Gainsborough, Stubbs and Guardi. For further information, see **www.holburne.org**.

The Thermae Bath Spa is a wonderful (if expensive) way of soothing muscles which ache after the exertions of the CW. Although the spa facilities are modern and glamorous, they provide a sense of connection to Bath's past: you will be doing exactly what people have been coming to Bath to do for 2000 years. The open-air rooftop pool, with its naturally warm, mineral-rich water, provides wonderful views of the city. For further information, see **www.thermaebathspa.com**.

KNIFE EDGE
Outdoor Guidebooks

We thought guidebooks were boring so we decided to change them. Mapping is better than 40 years ago. Graphics are better than 40 years ago. Photography is better than 40 years ago. So why have walking guidebooks remained the same?

Well our guidebooks are **different**:

► **We use Real Maps.** You know, the **1:25,000/1:50,000** scale maps that walkers actually use to navigate with. Not sketch maps that get you lost. Real maps make more work for us but we think it is worth it. You do not need to carry separate maps and you are less likely to get lost so we save you time!

► **Numbered Waypoints** on our Real Maps link to the walk descriptions, making routes easier to follow than traditional text-based guidebooks. No more wading through pages of boring words to find out where you are! You want to look at incredible scenery and not have your face stuck in a book all day. Right?

► **Colour, colour, colour.** Mountains and cliffs are **beautiful** so guidebooks should be too. We were fed up using guidebooks which were ugly and boring. When planning, we want to be **dazzled** with full-size colour pictures of the **magnificence** which awaits us! So our guidebooks fill every inch of the page with beauty: big, **spectacular** photos of mountains, etc.

► **More practical size.** Long enough to have Real Maps and large pictures but slim enough to fit in a pocket.

Now all that sounds great to us but we want to know if you like what we have done. So hit us with your feedback: good or bad. We are not too proud to change.

Follow us for trekking advice, book updates, discount coupons, articles and other interesting hiking stuff.

Facebook Groups

If you have any questions which are not answered in our books, then you can ask the author in one of our Facebook Groups. Updates to our books can be found in the topic sections of the groups.

The group for this book is 'The Cotswold Way'. Join by scanning the QR code below or use the following URL: **www.facebook.com/groups/CotswoldWay**

 www.knifeedgeoutdoor.com

 info@knifeedgeoutdoor.com

 @knifeedgeoutdoor

 @knifeedgeout

 @knifeedgeoutdoor